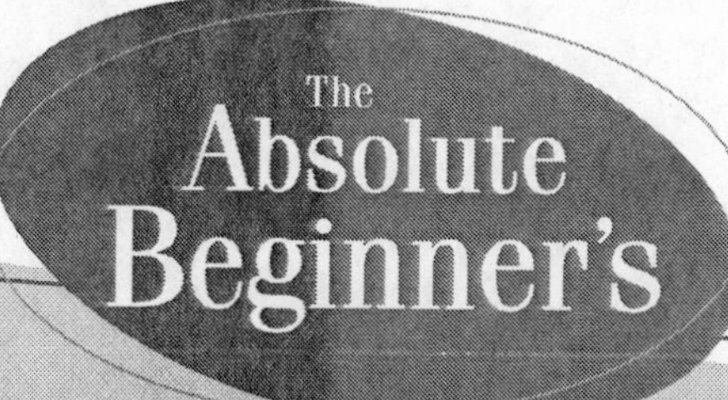


# COOKBOOK

## Or How Long Do I Cook a 3-Minute Egg?

Revised 3rd Edition

Jackie Eddy and Eleanor Clark

*To our husbands, Don and Trevor,*
*and to our eleven children*
*and seven children-in-law,*
*who were invaluable testers.*

*A special thanks to Sheri,*
*who not only helped with the testing*
*but who was our computer expert as well.*


Published in the United States by Three Rivers Press, an imprint of the Crown Publishing Group, a division of Random House, Inc., New York.
www.crownpublishing.com

THREE RIVERS PRESS and the Tugboat design are registered trademarks of Random House, Inc.

Originally published in the United States: by Prima Publishing, a division of Random House, Inc., Roseville, California, in 1995.

**Library of Congress Cataloging-in-Publication Data on file**

ISBN: 0-7615-3546-2

Printed in the United States of America

*Interior design by Susan Sugnet, Prima Design Group*

Third Edition

# Contents

# Introduction: Let's Start to Cook, But First...

This cookbook was written, as the title suggests, for the absolute beginner—the person who doesn't know how to cook but who still needs to eat; the one who asks, "How long do you cook a 3-minute egg?" By the way, the answer to that question isn't as simple as one might think: If you live at sea level (Boston, for instance) you cook it for 3 minutes, but if you live at a high altitude (Denver, for example) you cook it for 5 minutes! We have made the recipes *simple.* If you can read and can find the kitchen, the fridge, the stove, and the can opener, you are on your way not only to being a good cook but also to earning a reputation as a host or hostess nonpareil!

We are launching you on your cooking career with the easiest, best-tasting recipes in every category you require—dishes for breakfasts, brunches or light lunches, everyday suppers or fancy dinners, as well as desserts and snacks for in-between. We have presented a good selection of many old favorites; but lest the reader become bored, we have included enough innovative recipe ideas to capture the interest of even the experienced, seasoned cook.

A very important "trick" in the preparation of a good meal is having everything come out even—all ready at the same time. The easier the recipe, the easier this is to accomplish. We've done everything possible to simplify the preparation of the dishes in this book. We've taken no cooking skill for granted; we've explained everything step-by-step, and we've reduced the number of steps to the minimum.

We've assumed no familiarity on your part with the names of ingredients or utensils. We've taken care to call ingredients by the names under which you will find them at the supermarket, and in some cases we've even suggested particular brands. With each recipe we've listed the utensils you will need so you can see at a glance whether you're mechanically equipped to handle it. We have described or explained (as necessary) all the utensils in An Introduction to Utensils on page 335. If you are stocking up on kitchen equipment for the first time, you will find this list a handy guide to the essentials.

We have both been cooking for 25 years, and during this time we have learned many of the shortcuts, which are a boon for the beginner as well as any busy cook. There is nothing wrong with being a shortcut expert; if it tastes good, do it!

We have a few more general points of advice. The use of salt and pepper varies with individuals. Don't have too heavy a hand when a recipe calls for salt and pepper to taste. Add them carefully, tasting as you go until you are pleased with the end result. You can always add more. The experienced cook can usually rectify over-seasoning, but it is difficult for the beginner. See the section How to Measure on page 338 for help in getting the right amounts.

Have a light touch with spices and herbs as well, until you become more familiar with them, *and don't forget the parsley.* It is very important that a dish have eye appeal as well as taste appeal. Parsley and cherry tomatoes are the best garnishes to begin with. You can get into curls, rosettes, and other exotica when you are more comfortable in the kitchen.

Before you actually start preparing a particular dish, read the whole recipe through. Then assemble all your ingredients and utensils. Then start cooking. We have tried to present the recipes in a detailed and orderly way, warning you in advance, for example, that you will need to use the juice from a canned vegetable that you were just about to discard; but you will have your best chances of success if you have a clear idea *of exactly* what you will have to do through to the end.

You will see that in all the baking recipes, we have told you to turn the oven on right at the start of your preparations. This is very important. Always give ovens time to heat to the required temperature before you actually place the dish in the oven to bake.

Our last bit of advice: Learn to accept graciously these words, "That was the best food I've ever tasted!"

## More Absolute Beginner's Guides

*The Absolute Beginner's Guide to Mixing Drinks*

*The Absolute Beginner's Guide to Buying a House*

*The Absolute Beginner's Guide to Taking Great Photos*

# 1

# Eggs & Cheese

Boiled Eggs
Poached Eggs
Fried Eggs
Scrambled Eggs
French Toast
Omelette
Eggs Benedict
Toad in the Hole
Eggs in Toast Cups
Sunday Bacon & Cheese Breakfast
Pancakes
Whole Wheat Pancakes
Magic Bacon, Onion, & Cheese Quiche
Macaroni & Cheese
Never-Fail Cheese Soufflé

## Helpful Hints

1. Store eggs the same way they are packaged in the store, with the small point down; this keeps the yolks in the middle.
2. Add a little vinegar to the water when poaching eggs to prevent the egg whites from spreading.
3. One-fourth pound Cheddar cheese yields 1 cup grated cheese.

## BOILED EGGS

*Every experienced cook has to know how to cook an egg. If you have to cook for yourself, it is essential to learn how to deal with eggs. There are countless methods of preparation. We will try to cover the major ones in this section, starting with the most basic, the boiled egg, and gradually moving through to the "gourmet" version, which is Eggs Benedict. All eggs used in the following recipes are* large-size eggs.

**1 egg, room temperature**

Utensils needed

**small saucepan**

1. Immerse the egg in a small saucepan of cold water.
2. Bring water to a boil over high heat.
3. As soon as the water bubbles, turn heat down so that water stays simmering or bubbling gently.
4. *Cover* the saucepan and start timing.
5. For a soft-boiled egg, simmer for 5 minutes. For a hard-boiled egg, simmer for 12 minutes. The timing will depend on how you like your egg. And, believe it or not, the altitude at which you are cooking makes a difference! This timing is for a high altitude. A soft-boiled egg cooked at sea level will take a full 2 minutes less cooking time and a hard-boiled egg will take 3 minutes less.
6. When the egg is cooked, drain off the hot water and immediately rinse with cold water to prevent the egg from cooking further. This also makes the shell easier to peel. (Peel by cracking the shell gently against a hard surface.)

*Serves 1.*

Note: *If you inadvertently overcook your egg, use it to make a delicious Easy Egg Salad sandwich* *(see page 89)**.*

# POACHED EGGS

**1 teaspoon white vinegar**

**1 egg**

Utensils needed

**small saucepan**

**slotted spoon**

1. Fill a small saucepan two-thirds full with water.
2. Add vinegar.
3. Bring water to a boil over high heat.
4. When water is boiling, take a spoon and stir so the water moves in a gently circular motion. There will be an indentation in the center of the water—that is where you will drop the egg when you have cracked it open.
5. Crack the egg by hitting it sharply across its widest part on the side of the saucepan. Drop the egg into the swirling water.
6. Turn the heat down to simmer and cook the egg for 2 or 3 minutes until the white part is solid.
7. Remove the egg with a slotted spoon, holding it above the saucepan for a couple of seconds so the water can drip off.

*Serves 1.*

# FRIED EGGS

**1 tablespoon butter**

**1 egg**

**½ teaspoon water**

**Salt and pepper**

Utensils needed

**small frying pan (with lid)**

**spoon**

**spatula**

1. Place frying pan over low to medium heat and add butter. When it has melted, the butter should cover the bottom of the pan generously. Add more butter if necessary. Heat butter until it starts to foam.
2. Immediately break the egg into the frying pan.
3. As soon as the white is set, tilt the skillet a bit and, using a spoon, collect some of the butter and spoon over the egg two or three times so that the top cooks as well.
4. If you like the yolk fairly well cooked, add the ½ teaspoon of water and immediately place a lid over the pan.* This will reflect the heat onto the top of the egg.
5. Remove the egg to a *warm* plate with the spatula, and sprinkle with salt and pepper just before serving.

*Serves 1.*

* Instead of adding the water, you may turn the egg over gently with a spatula. However, you may find it difficult to do this without breaking the yolk; for beginner cooks especially, this is *not* an easy over!

# SCRAMBLED EGGS

**2 eggs**

**Salt and pepper**

**1 tablespoon butter**

Utensils needed

**small deep bowl**

**egg beater, wire whisk, or fork**

**small frying pan**

**spatula**

1. Break the eggs into the bowl, sprinkle with salt and pepper to taste, and beat with an egg beater, a wire whisk, or a fork until very well mixed.
2. Melt butter over low heat in a small frying pan (no larger than 8 inches).
3. Add the eggs to the frying pan and stir constantly with the spatula as they cook and thicken so the butter and the eggs mix well. The longer you cook them, the drier they become. Most people find them more palatable if they are more on the moist side rather than dry, so remove them when they still are a little shiny on top.
4. Remove to a warm plate.

*Serves 1.*

*Suggested Accompaniments:* Midweek–toast and jam. Weekend–bacon and sausage, cherry tomatoes or broiled tomato halves, muffins.

# FRENCH TOAST

**1 egg**

**1 teaspoon milk**

**1 to 1½ slices white bread**

**1½ teaspoons butter**

Utensils needed

**shallow bowl**

**egg beater or whisk**

**small frying pan**

**spatula**

1. Break the egg into a shallow bowl and add milk. Beat well with a whisk or egg beater.
2. Dip bread in egg mixture, making sure both sides get covered with egg. Let moisture soak in a bit, but not enough that the bread starts to fall apart.
3. Melt butter over medium heat in the frying pan.
4. Fry the soaked bread in the frying pan until golden brown on the bottom. Turn with a spatula and cook the other side until golden brown.

*Serves 1.*

*Serving Suggestion:* You may sprinkle the French toast with a mixture of equal amounts of sugar and cinnamon or serve with maple syrup.

# OMELETTE

*The secret of a good omelette is speed and constant attention.*

**2 eggs**

**2 teaspoons cold water**

**Sprinkle of salt**

**Sprinkle of pepper**

**1 tablespoon butter**

Utensils needed

**medium nonstick frying pan or omelette pan**

**small bowl**

**wire whisk or fork**

**broad spatula**

1. Place the frying pan over medium heat.
2. Set your serving plate in the oven to warm.
3. Break the eggs into a bowl and add water, salt, and pepper.
4. Beat the eggs well with the whisk or a fork until there is a high froth on top.
5. Spear the butter with a fork. Touch the hot pan with the butter, which should sizzle on contact.
6. When all the butter is melted, tip and roll the frying pan so that the butter flows over the bottom and part-way up the sides.
7. *Immediately* pour the eggs in all at once. Working quickly, shake the pan vigorously back and forth three or four times with your left hand.
8. Prick the middle of the omelette three or four times with a fork held in your right hand (if you're left-handed, switch

hands!), then go all around the edges gently with the fork, tilting the pan with your left hand to allow the uncooked part to flow down underneath (where the heat is). Continue this procedure until there is no more "runny" egg.

9. With a broad spatula, lift one-half of the omelette and flip over onto second half. Now gently nudge or slide the folded omelette onto the warm serving plate.

*Serves 1.*

*Serving Suggestion: You* may dress up the omelette any way you like—with chopped ham, cheese, bacon, mushrooms, and so forth—by placing the filling (chopped small to heat quickly) down the center of the omelette just before you fold it over.

# EGGS BENEDICT

*For your first venture into this dish, you should use a Hollandaise sauce mix; most supermarkets carry this, and you simply follow directions on the package. If you want to make your own, however, the (Almost) Hollandaise Sauce that is found on page 10 is an excellent substitute for the tricky real thing!*

**1 tablespoon butter**

**2 English muffins, split**

**2 teaspoons oil**

**4 slices Canadian back bacon**

**4 poached eggs (see page 3)**

**Hollandaise sauce—packaged mix or following recipe**

Utensils needed

**medium frying pan**

**large saucepan**

**small saucepan**

**slotted spoon**

1. Turn broiler on.
2. Butter muffin halves and broil about 4 to 6 inches from heat until golden brown.
3. Heat the oil in the frying pan and add bacon.
4. Cook over medium heat until the bacon starts to brown; turn, and gently brown the other side.
5. Place bacon on muffin halves and keep warm.
6. Bring water for poached eggs to a boil in a large saucepan.
7. While water is heating, make the Hollandaise sauce.

8. Prepare the poached eggs.
9. Place drained poached eggs on top of bacon slices and spoon Hollandaise sauce on top.

*Serves 2.*

Note: *For a very attractive garnish, decorate the plate with two or three cherry tomatoes and a sprig of parsley.*

## (Almost) Hollandaise Sauce

**¾ cup mayonnaise**

**¼ cup sour cream**

**1 teaspoon lemon juice**

**½ teaspoon Dijon mustard**

**Sprinkle of salt**

**Sprinkle of pepper**

Utensils needed

**small saucepan**

1. Combine all the ingredients in a small saucepan.
2. When well mixed, heat gently over very low heat. The mixture does not need to be cooked, just heated.

# TOAD IN THE HOLE

*This makes an excellent supper dish.*

**1 pound breakfast sausages**

**¾ cup all-purpose flour**

**½ teaspoon salt**

**2 eggs**

**1 cup milk**

Utensils needed

**8-inch square baking dish**

**2 small bowls**

1. Place sausages in the baking dish and place in *cold* oven.
2. Turn the oven on to 450 degrees F.
3. Combine flour and salt in a bowl.
4. While the oven is heating, beat together the eggs and milk in the second bowl. Add this mixture to the flour and salt, and beat well with a fork.
5. When oven is at the required temperature (usually ranges have a red light that goes off to indicate this), remove the dish from the oven, pour off 1 tablespoon of fat, and turn sausages over.
6. Pour the batter over the sausages while sausages and pan are still hot. Return pan to oven.
7. Reduce oven temperature to 425 degrees and bake for 30 to 35 minutes. The batter will puff up, will be brown and crusty, and should be served at once.

*Serves 3 to 4.*

*Suggested Accompaniment:* A Tossed Green Salad (see page 91) or corn would complete this meal perfectly.

# EGGS IN TOAST CUPS

*The cups may be made a few days in advance, making this a very easy dish. When the eggs are cooked, remove them to a warm plate and surround with cooked ham, bacon, or sausages–and don't forget the sprig of parsley!*

**2 thin slices sandwich bread**

**Melted butter or margarine**

**2 eggs, room temperature**

Utensils needed

**muffin tins or custard cups**

1. Turn oven on to 325 degrees F.
2. Trim crusts from bread, and brush both sides with melted butter.
3. Place bread firmly in muffin cups.
4. Bake at 325 degrees for 15 minutes or until bread cups are golden brown. Remove from oven.
5. Just before you are ready to serve, heat the oven to 350 degrees F.
6. Reheat the toast cups slightly if you have made them ahead.
7. Break an egg into each warm toast cup.
8. Bake for 15 minutes. (If you have taken the eggs directly from the refrigerator, allow an extra 2 to 3 minutes.)

*Serves 2.*

*Variation:* An alternative to the melted butter is a combination of equal portions of soft butter and mayonnaise. Spread mixture on one side of bread only. When you are placing them in muffin tins, have the spread side down. Bake as above.

## SUNDAY BACON & CHEESE BREAKFAST

*This needn't be specifically for Sundays nor for breakfast. Add a Tossed Green Salad (see page 91), and it makes an excellent brunch or supper dish.*

**4 slices bacon**

**4 slices white bread**

**Butter or margarine**

**1½ cups grated sharp Cheddar cheese**

**1 cup skim milk**

**1 beaten egg**

**½ teaspoon seasoned salt**

**½ teaspoon white pepper**

**1 tablespoon grated onion**

**1 teaspoon Worcestershire sauce**

Utensils needed

**grater**

**medium frying pan**

**toaster**

**9- by 5-inch loaf pan**

**small bowl**

1. Cook the bacon in the frying pan and set aside.
2. Toast the bread, butter it, and cut lengthwise into thirds.
3. Sprinkle one-third of the grated cheese over the bottom of a loaf pan.
4. Place six fingers of toast on top of the cheese.
5. Sprinkle the second third of the cheese on top of the toast and lay the remaining six fingers of toast on top. Sprinkle the rest of the cheese over this.

6. Combine the remaining ingredients, except for bacon, in a small bowl. Pour over the toast and cheese in the pan.
7. Break the cooked bacon into bits, and sprinkle on top.
8. Let stand for 15 to 20 minutes.
9. Turn oven on to 375 degrees F. When oven is ready (indicator light will go off), place pan in oven and bake for 25 minutes.

*Serves 2 to 3.*

*Serving Suggestion:* If you plan to serve this to guests, the addition of a broiled halved tomato would make a very attractive plate.

## PANCAKES

*Our best advice is to buy a package of pancake mix and follow the directions on the package. However, if you have your mouth set for pancakes and no mix in the house, simply follow this recipe. The thinner the batter, the thinner the pancakes. If you like thick pancakes, cut down on the milk a bit.*

**1½ cups all-purpose flour**

**1 tablespoon sugar**

**1 tablespoon baking powder**

**½ teaspoon salt**

**1 egg**

**1¾ cups milk**

**2 tablespoons oil**

Utensils needed

**2 large bowls**

**egg beater or fork**

**large frying pan or griddle**

**spatula**

1. Sift the dry ingredients together in a large bowl.
2. In a separate bowl, beat egg, milk, and oil together with a beater or fork, then stir into dry ingredients until almost smooth.
3. Let the batter sit while you prepare the frying pan or griddle.
4. If your frying pan is electric, set it at 400 degrees F. For a stovetop frying pan, turn the element to just above medium. Heat the pan. (The best test to see if the pan is ready is to drop a bit of water from your finger–the drop should "bounce.")

5. Lightly grease the pan with additional vegetable oil (butter will burn), then pour in some batter—the amount will depend on how large you want your pancakes (one-quarter cup of batter makes a good size).
6. When the tops of the pancakes are covered with bubbles and the edges are beginning to look dry, turn the pancakes over with a spatula. They will take only half the time to cook on the second side.
7. Serve with the syrup of your choice.

*Serves 4.*

*Variation:* For blueberry pancakes: Sprinkle a few fresh or frozen blueberries on top of the uncooked side of the pancake before you turn it. Don't add blueberries to the batter when you are mixing it—the batter will turn blue!

# WHOLE WHEAT PANCAKES

**¾ cup whole wheat flour**

**¼ cup all-purpose flour**

**2 tablespoons baking powder**

**2 tablespoons sugar**

**½ teaspoon salt**

**1 egg, beaten**

**1¼ cups milk**

**3 tablespoons vegetable oil**

Utensils needed

**large bowl**

**medium bowl**

**electric frying pan or nonstick skillet**

1. Combine all of the dry ingredients together in a large bowl. (It is best to sift them into the bowl but not necessary.)
2. In a separate bowl, combine egg, milk, and oil.
3. Stir the wet ingredients into the dry ingredients until the dry ingredients are moistened. (Don't worry about a few lumps.)
4. Let the batter sit while you prepare an electric frying pan or nonstick skillet.
5. If your frying pan is electric, set it at 400 degrees F. For a stovetop frying pan, turn the element to just above medium. Heat the pan. (The best test to see if the pan is ready is to drop a bit of water from your finger–the drop should "bounce.")

6. Lightly grease the pan with additional vegetable oil (butter will burn), then drop the batter into the skillet from a large spoon or measuring cup—the amount will depend on how large you want your pancakes (one-quarter cup of batter makes a good size).
7. When the tops of the pancakes are covered with bubbles and the edges are beginning to look dry, turn the pancakes over with a spatula. They will only take half the time to cook on the second side.
8. Serve with the syrup of your choice.

*Serves 4 (makes about 12 4-inch pancakes).*

*Suggested Accompaniments:* Sour cream and berry topping. Combine ½ cup nonfat sour cream and 2 tablespoons maple syrup. Spoon some of this mixture over each pancake and top with berries of your choice.

# MAGIC BACON, ONION, & CHEESE QUICHE

*We've called this magic because you don't have to be bothered rolling out a crust; you simply add the ingredients in the proper order and the crust mysteriously goes to the bottom and the filling rises to the top.*

**1 teaspoon vegetable oil**

**6 strips bacon**

**1 small bunch green onions**

**1 cup grated Cheddar cheese**

**1½ cups milk**

**¾ cup Bisquick baking mix**

**3 eggs**

**1 teaspoon salt**

**¼ teaspoon pepper**

Utensils needed

**grater**

**10-inch pie plate**

**large frying pan**

**chopping knife**

**large bowl**

**hand mixer or blender**

1. Heat oven to 400 degrees F.
2. Lightly grease the pie plate with the oil.
3. In the frying pan, fry the bacon until crisp. Crumble.
4. Chop the onions, using all the white and a bit of the green.
5. Spread onions, cheese, and bacon in the bottom of the pie plate.

6. Combine the milk, Bisquick, eggs, salt, and pepper in a mixing bowl. Beat for 1 minute with a hand mixer until smooth. (You may pour these ingredients into a blender if you have one and mix at high speed for 15 seconds.)
7. Pour into the pie plate.
8. Bake about 30 to 35 minutes until golden brown and a knife inserted into the center comes out clean.
9. Let stand for 5 minutes before cutting.

*Serves 6.*

## MACARONI & CHEESE

*This is a dish your mother made you eat when you were a child; but you never really liked it until you grew up, and now you just "have to have some" every once in a while!*

**2 quarts water**

**2 teaspoons salt**

**1 teaspoon oil**

**1 package (8 ounces) ready-cut macaroni**

**1 can (10 ounces) Cheddar cheese soup**

**¾ cup milk**

**2 cups grated sharp Cheddar cheese**

**½ teaspoon Worcestershire sauce**

**Pinch of dry mustard powder**

**⅓ cup bread crumbs**

Utensils needed

**grater**

**large saucepan**

**colander**

**2-quart casserole or 13- by 9- by 2-inch baking dish**

**can opener**

1. Turn oven on to 400 degrees F.
2. In a large saucepan, bring the water to a rolling boil, then add the salt and oil. (The oil will help prevent the macaroni from boiling over.)
3. Add the macaroni and cook uncovered at a full rolling boil until tender, stirring occasionally (about 7 to 9 minutes).

4. Drain in a colander, rinse with cold water, and drain again.
5. Grease the casserole or baking dish.
6. In a large bowl or the saucepan, blend the undiluted soup, milk, and 1¾ cups of the grated cheese, saving ¼ cup for the top.
7. Add the Worcestershire sauce and mustard and mix well. Stir in the macaroni.
8. Pour into the greased baking dish.
9. Sprinkle bread crumbs and the remaining ¼ cup cheese on top.
10. Bake for 20 to 25 minutes or until sauce is bubbly and crumbs are browned.

*Serves 6.*

Note: *Crushed cracker crumbs may be substituted for bread crumbs.*

# NEVER-FAIL CHEESE SOUFFLÉ

*Mention* soufflé *to a beginning cook, and it conjures up thoughts of the failure factor and what to do with a fallen soufflé! This one really is foolproof, and even though it may lose some of its height when removed from the oven, it loses none of its texture because of the tapioca. Don't hesitate to buy minute tapioca; you will use it up quickly (see Busy Day Stew, page 134), and we guarantee you will want to make this soufflé again and again.*

**6 ounces Cheddar cheese**

**1 cup milk**

**3 tablespoons minute tapioca**

**1 teaspoon salt**

**1 teaspoon oil**

**3 large eggs**

Utensils needed

**grater**
**small saucepan**
**soufflé dish or 1-quart casserole dish**
**large bowl**
**small bowl**
**electric or hand mixer or wire whisk**
**spatula**
**ovenproof dish slightly larger than soufflé dish**

1. Preheat the oven to 350 degrees F.
2. Grate the cheese and set aside.
3. Combine milk and tapioca in the small saucepan.
4. Heat to a full rolling boil (bubbles break the surface), stirring constantly.

5. Remove from heat and add grated cheese and salt, stirring until smooth.
6. Lightly grease the soufflé dish.
7. Separate the eggs, placing yolks in the large bowl and whites in the small bowl.*
8. With a clean whisk or a mixer, beat the egg whites until stiff peaks form.
9. Beat the egg yolks until thick and pale.
10. Gradually add the tapioca and cheese mixture to the egg yolks.
11. With a spatula, gently fold in the stiffly beaten egg whites, then pour into the soufflé dish.
12. Place this dish in a larger dish containing 1 inch of water and bake at 350 degrees for 50 to 60 minutes. The top should be golden brown when cooked. (Do not open the oven door until soufflé is ready.)
13. Serve immediately if possible, but the soufflé can be held for 10 to 15 minutes by turning off the oven and opening the oven door slightly.

*Serves 6.*

* To separate an egg, hold it over the bowl that will be used to catch the white and crack the shell in the middle (crossways) by tapping it gently on the rim of the bowl. Immediately turn the egg upright, with the largest part of the shell at the bottom. Remove the top shell, allowing one-half of the white to drip into the bowl. The yolk will stay in the bottom because it is heavier. Now pour the yolk carefully into the empty top shell, which will allow more of the white to drip into the bowl. Repeat this transferring of the yolk back and forth until you are left with just the yolk. It doesn't matter if a bit of the white sticks to the yolk but it does matter if even a speck of yolk spills into the white, because then the white will not whip. Should this happen, use an empty shell to remove the bit of yolk. (The yolk will adhere better to the inside of the shell than to a spoon.)

# 2

# Breads & Muffins

Cheesy Garlic Bread
Whole Wheat Baking Powder Biscuits
Easy Cheese Bread
Whole Wheat Coffee-Can Bread
Easy Banana Bread
Butterscotch Pecan Buns
Big & Beautiful Blueberry Muffins
Banana Bran Muffins
Sharon's Feta or Blue Cheese Buns
Cinnamon Coffee Cake

## Helpful Hints

1. When baking loaf cakes, let the batter sit in the pan for 20 minutes before baking. This will lessen the size of the crack in the top so typical of loaf cakes.
2. Soft bread cuts more easily with a slightly heated bread knife.

# CHEESY GARLIC BREAD

*Everyone has his or her own version of this popular favorite, so here's ours. It's a good idea to cut the loaf a few hours or even the day before, wrap it, and freeze it; you will find it easier to spread the butter on the frozen surface. We always keep French bread halves in the freezer for emergencies.*

**¼ pound butter**

**1 clove garlic**

**1 loaf French bread**

**Processed cheese slices**

Utensils needed

**small bowl**

**garlic press**

**bread knife**

1. Several hours or the day before you wish to serve the bread, prepare a garlic butter as follows: Take the butter out of the refrigerator and let it stand at room temperature in a small bowl to soften. Peel the garlic clove and put it through a garlic press. (If you do not have a press, simply chop the clove finely.) Mix garlic into the soft butter.
2. Cover the dish tightly and set it aside, not in the refrigerator (you want to keep the butter spreadable). It will take a few hours for the garlic flavor to penetrate the butter.
3. About 30 minutes before serving, cut the French loaf in half lengthwise; spread each side liberally with garlic butter.
4. Toast the bread halves under the broiler until golden brown. Watch carefully that the toast does not burn.
5. Remove the bread from under the broiler. Lay cheese slices along one half.

6. Put halves together to re-form the loaf. Wrap in tin foil.
7. Turn the oven to 350 degrees F (no preheating necessary). Warm the garlic bread in the oven for about 25 minutes.
8. Remove from oven, loosen the tin foil, and cut the bread into 2-inch strips. Serve in the tin foil.

*Serves 6 to 8.*

*Variations:* Parmesan cheese may be substituted for the cheese slices. Just sprinkle Parmesan on each half of the bread before placing it under the broiler. If you are rushed, substitute ½ teaspoon garlic powder for the clove of garlic, mix it into the butter, and spread immediately.

# WHOLE WHEAT BAKING POWDER BISCUITS

*Hot biscuits, fresh from the oven–sure to impress (even yourself!).*

**Butter or nonstick cooking spray**

**1½ cups whole wheat flour**

**½ teaspoon salt**

**2½ teaspoons baking powder**

**½ teaspoon baking soda**

**1 cup sour cream**

Utensils needed

**large cookie sheet**

**mixing bowl**

**sharp knife**

1. Heat oven to 450 degrees F.
2. Grease the cookie sheet.
3. Combine all the dry ingredients in a mixing bowl.
4. Stir in the sour cream. Blend with a fork or your fingers only until all the flour mixture is incorporated into a ball of dough.
5. Sprinkle a little extra flour on a clean countertop and transfer the ball of dough to countertop. Using your fingers, press dough to a thickness of ¾ to 1 inch.
6. Take a sharp knife and cut dough into diagonals about 2 inches in width. Place on the greased cookie sheet.
7. Bake in the oven at 450 degrees for 10 to 12 minutes.

*Makes about 10 biscuits.*

Note: *If you're feeling adventurous, for a change of shape use a medium-size tumbler to cut round biscuits. Scraps may be baked as is; they make great nibblers.*

*Variation:* For traditional baking powder biscuits, substitute all-purpose (white) flour for the whole wheat flour or use ¾ cup whole wheat and ¾ cup all-purpose flour.

# EASY CHEESE BREAD

*Hard to believe something this easy can be so good-tasting. It's a favorite for barbecues. It may be made ahead of time: Cool, slice, butter, wrap in foil, and freeze until serving time, then thaw and reheat.*

**Butter or nonstick cooking spray**

**1 cup grated Cheddar cheese**

**3 cups Bisquick baking mix**

**1 cup milk**

**1 tablespoon parsley**

**⅛ teaspoon garlic salt (optional)**

Utensils needed

**grater**

**9- by 5-inch loaf pan**

**mixing bowl**

1. Heat the oven to 400 degrees F.
2. Grease the loaf pan.
3. Combine cheese with other ingredients in a mixing bowl, stirring only enough to blend.
4. Transfer to the greased loaf pan.
5. Bake at 400 degrees for 40 to 50 minutes.
6. When baked, leave in the pan and cool on a rack for 10 minutes before removing the loaf from the pan.

*Serves 6.*

*Variation:* Substitute 1 whole can (12 ounces) of your favorite alcoholic or nonalcoholic beer (room temperature) for the 1 cup of milk called for in the above recipe.

## WHOLE WHEAT COFFEE-CAN BREAD

**½ cup warm water**

**3 tablespoons sugar**

**1 package dry yeast**

**1 can (13 ounces) evaporated milk, at room temperature**

**1 teaspoon salt**

**2 tablespoons oil**

**2 cups all-purpose flour**

**2 cups whole wheat flour**

**Butter or nonstick cooking spray**

Utensils needed

**large bowl**

**small bowl**

**wooden spoon**

**2 1-pound coffee cans**

1. Place warm water in a large mixing bowl and stir in *1 tablespoon* sugar until sugar is dissolved.
2. Sprinkle yeast on top and let sit for 15 minutes.
3. In the small mixing bowl, combine the evaporated milk, salt, the remaining 2 tablespoons of sugar, and oil and stir until sugar is dissolved.
4. When yeast is ready, stir down (it will have risen a bit), then stir in the evaporated milk mixture.
5. Combine the two flours and stir into above mixture. The dough will be a little stiff–you might have to use your "paw" to mix in all the flour, but a wooden spoon should do the job.

6. Grease the coffee cans and lids well.*
7. Divide the dough in half and place each half in the well-greased coffee can.
8. Place lids on top of cans and wait until the lid "pops." This usually takes 1½ to 2 hours.
9. About 1¼ hours after you have put the bread to rise, turn the oven on to 350 degrees F. You want the oven to be ready, because the bread must go in the oven *as soon as the lids pop.* When this happens, place bread in the oven and bake for 45 minutes.
10. Remove from can and let cool on a cake rack. You may brush some melted butter on the tops of the loaves if you want them to have a shiny appearance, but this is not essential.

*Makes 2 loaves.*

* Instead of greasing, spraying the can with a vegetable cooking spray works really well—the bread never sticks. Be sure to spray the lid, too.

# EASY BANANA BREAD

*Not only is this one of the best and easiest banana breads around but it is "Heart Smart" when you use light or lowfat salad dressing. See "Helpful Hint for Bananas" following the recipe.*

**½ cup Miracle Whip Light Salad Dressing**

**1 large egg**

**3 medium-size ripe (even overripe) bananas, mashed**

**1½ cups all-purpose flour**

**1 cup sugar**

**½ cup chopped walnuts or pecans (optional)**

**1 teaspoon baking soda**

**1 teaspoon salt**

**Butter or nonstick cooking spray**

Utensils needed

**small bowl**

**medium bowl**

**9- by 5-inch loaf pan**

1. Preheat oven to 350 degrees F.
2. In a small bowl, combine salad dressing, egg, and mashed bananas.
3. In a medium bowl, combine flour, sugar, nuts, baking soda, and salt.
4. Stir the dry ingredients into the banana mixture, mixing only until dry ingredients are incorporated.
5. Empty batter into a 9- by 5-inch greased loaf pan (no need to flour pan).

6. Bake for 60 to 70 minutes or until a toothpick inserted in the middle comes out clean.
7. Let stand 10 minutes, then remove from pan.
8. Cool before slicing. (If you just *can't* wait, go ahead and slice a piece when it's still warm!)

*Makes 1 loaf.*

*Helpful Hint for Bananas:* It seems that bananas never come out even. You're always left with one or two overripe, black, or mottled bananas (they age even faster than people!). Solution? Keep a large baggie in the freezer and pop in unpeeled overripe bananas as they come along. The next time you need bananas for a recipe, simply peel the bananas while they are still frozen, then thaw and mash them.

# BUTTERSCOTCH PECAN BUNS

*This recipe, which uses Pillsbury bread sticks, is so good. We used Mrs. Richardson's Butterscotch Sauce, but any butterscotch or caramel ice cream topping will do.*

**⅓ cup butterscotch ice cream topping***

**2 tablespoons melted butter or margarine**

**⅓ cup pecan halves**

**1 package Pillsbury bread sticks**

Utensils needed

**9-inch round cake pan or pie plate**

1. Preheat oven to 350 degrees F.
2. In a 9-inch round baking pan (cake pan), stir together the butterscotch sauce and melted butter.
3. Arrange pecan halves on top of butter and butterscotch sauce mixture.
4. Separate bread sticks, but do not uncoil.
5. Arrange the individual dough coils in baking pan (on top of pecans) and bake for 20 to 25 minutes or until golden brown.
6. Let stand for 2 to 3 minutes before removing from pan.
7. To remove from pan, place a plate or platter over top of pan and turn pan upside down. Serve warm.

*Makes 8 buns.*

* You can substitute 3 tablespoons of corn syrup for the ⅓ cup of butterscotch ice cream topping.

# BIG & BEAUTIFUL BLUEBERRY MUFFINS

**Butter or nonstick cooking spray**

**1¾ cups all-purpose flour**

**¼ cup sugar**

**1 tablespoon baking powder**

**1 teaspoon cinnamon**

**¾ teaspoon salt**

**1 egg**

**1 cup milk**

**¼ cup melted margarine**

**1 cup blueberries (fresh or frozen)**

Utensils needed

**large muffin tins**

**large bowl**

**small bowl**

**wooden spoon**

1. Turn oven to 425 degrees F.
2. Grease the muffin tins well or spray with a vegetable cooking oil.
3. Sift together the flour, sugar, baking powder, cinnamon, and salt into a large bowl.
4. In the smaller bowl, beat the egg, milk, and melted margarine together with a wooden spoon, then stir lightly into dry ingredients.
5. Gently fold in the berries. (Never overmix muffins—just enough to absorb the flour.)

6. Fill the well-greased muffin tins three-quarters full.
7. Bake at 425 degrees for 20 minutes.

*Makes 6 large muffins.*

*Variations:*

1. Sprinkle muffin tops with a mixture of equal parts of cinnamon and sugar before placing in oven.
2. If you like the "giant" muffins found in muffin specialty shops, use custard cups to bake the muffins. Be sure to spray or grease them well first.

# BANANA BRAN MUFFINS

*It is fairly common knowledge that buttermilk makes the very best bran muffins. Once you make these muffins, you'll be hooked. They are the best we've ever eaten—and very easy to make.*

**Butter or nonstick cooking spray**

**1 medium banana**

**3 cups bran (the natural bran, not the cereal)**

**3 cups buttermilk**

**2 eggs, slightly beaten**

**½ cup vegetable oil**

**2½ cups all-purpose flour**

**1 cup sugar**

**2½ teaspoons baking soda**

**¾ teaspoon salt**

Utensils needed

**large muffin tins**

**chopping knife**

**large bowl**

**medium bowl**

1. Heat oven to 400 degrees F.
2. Grease the muffin tins well or spray them with nonstick cooking spray.
3. Dice the banana into tiny squares (you should have 1 cup of finely chopped banana).
4. In a large bowl, mix bran, buttermilk, eggs, oil, and diced banana.

5. In a medium bowl, combine the flour, sugar, baking soda, and salt. Stir together to mix well.
6. Add the dry mixture to the first mixture in the large bowl, stirring just enough to absorb all the flour. Do not overmix.
7. Fill the well-greased muffin tins about two-thirds to three-quarters full. Don't use the paper baking cups; they will stick.
8. Bake for 20 minutes.

*Makes 2½ dozen large muffins.*

Note: *If you want to always have buttermilk on hand, buy a can of dry buttermilk mix. (Substitute 6 tablespoons buttermilk mix and 3 cups cold water to make the 3 cups buttermilk.)*

*Variations:* If you don't like the bran and banana combination, substitute raisins for the chopped banana or even dates—or a combination of raisins and dates—but don't exceed 1 cup.

# SHARON'S FETA OR BLUE CHEESE BUNS

*Adding cheese is a great way to dress up dinner buns for special occasions. If you want to turn them into a quick and easy (and terrific) appetizer, cut the biscuits into quarters and put in a round, greased pie pan, just touching each other, and pour the cheese-butter mixture over the top. Blue cheese works best for the appetizer and feta is best for dinner buns.*

**2 tablespoons butter**

**2 tablespoons crumbled feta or blue cheese**

**1 package Refrigerated Country Biscuits or buttermilk biscuits**

Utensils needed

**small saucepan**

**8- or 9-inch round cake pan or pie plate**

1. Turn oven to 450 degrees F.
2. Melt butter in small saucepan, add cheese, and stir until smooth (drier feta may have little "curds" but will work just fine).
3. Place biscuits in a greased 8- or 9-inch round cake pan and spoon cheese mixture over top.
4. Bake for 10 minutes or until browned.

*Makes 8 buns.*

# CINNAMON COFFEE CAKE

*The marvelous aroma that wafts through your kitchen will have your friends drooling. Serve this coffee cake piping hot from the oven, and make sure you keep the basic ingredients on hand so you can make it up on the spur of the moment. Great for coffee parties, brunches, and late-night snacks.*

**¼ cup butter, softened**

**1 cup sugar**

**2 eggs**

**1 teaspoon vanilla**

**1 teaspoon baking powder**

**1 teaspoon baking soda**

**½ teaspoon salt**

**2 cups all-purpose flour**

**1 cup sour cream**

**4 tablespoons brown sugar**

**1 tablespoon cinnamon**

**Butter or nonstick cooking spray**

Utensils needed

**large bowl**

**electric or hand mixer**

**small bowl**

**9- by 5-inch loaf pan or 9-inch square cake pan**

1. Heat oven to 375 degrees F.
2. Beat butter and sugar in the large mixing bowl until creamy.
3. Mix in eggs and vanilla.
4. In a small bowl, mix baking powder, baking soda, salt, and all-purpose flour.

5. A little bit at a time, add dry ingredients and sour cream alternately to creamed mixture, beating in between additions. The batter will be thick.
6. Mix brown sugar and cinnamon together in the small bowl for topping.
7. Grease the pan or spray with a vegetable cooking oil.
8. Empty half the batter into the pan and smooth it out.
9. Sprinkle half the topping over batter.
10. Add remainder of batter and sprinkle with remaining topping mix.
11. Bake at 375 degrees for 30 minutes if using a cake pan or at the same temperature for 40 minutes if using a loaf pan.

*Makes 1 cake.*

*Variation:* This batter also makes delicious muffins. Fill greased muffin tins two-thirds full and bake at 375 degrees for 15 to 20 minutes.

# 3

# Appetizers & Hors D'oeuvres

"No Cook" Antipasto
Cheese Wafers
Crab & Cheese Platter
Savory Ritz Bites
Mexican Pie Plate Dip
Cranberry & Feta Pinwheels
Nachos (Hot & Simple)
Nachos with Cheese Dip
Guacamole
Potato Skins
Taco Dip
Cream Cheese Toppings
Spinach Dip in Hollowed-Out Loaf
Hummus with Toasted Pita Triangles
Baked Whole Garlic
English Muffin Wedges
David's Cocktail Almonds
Bruschetta
Hot Artichoke Dip

## "NO COOK" ANTIPASTO

*This is the very easiest antipasto for a beginner to tackle. If you know how to chop and stir, you can make this delicious appetizer, which will keep for two months under refrigeration. With a box of crackers on the shelf and a jar of antipasto in the refrigerator, you are never stuck for a quick hors d'oeuvre.*

**1 small bottle ketchup**

**1 bottle (10 ounces) chili sauce**

**1 jar (12 ounces) sweet mixed pickles**

**1 jar (10 ounces) stuffed green olives**

**1 can (10 ounces) black olives**

**1 can (10 ounces) whole mushrooms**

### Helpful Hints

1. Dip water chestnuts in Parmesan cheese, then wrap each in a slice of bacon. Secure with a toothpick and bake at 400 degrees F until the bacon is cooked. Delicious!
2. Never wash mushrooms, as they become watery. They are grown in sterile soil and thus are not "dirty." Brush them with a soft cloth or paper towel or mushroom brush. If the mushrooms are slightly old and discolored, peel them.
3. Make an easy mushroom filling by mixing grated onion or chopped green onion into mayonnaise. Bake at 425 degrees F for about 5 to 7 minutes.
4. Make a quick sauce for cooked meatballs by heating together a 12-ounce jar of chili sauce and a 10-ounce jar of grape jelly. When jelly is melted, pour over meatballs and simmer until meatballs are well heated through.

**1 jar (5 ounces) cocktail onions, smallest size**

**2 cans (6.5 ounces each) tuna**

Utensils needed

**can opener**

**large bowl**

**chopping knife**

**sterilized jars for storage**

1. Empty ketchup and chili sauce into a large bowl.
2. Drain the pickles, olives, and mushrooms well.
3. Chop into fairly small pieces and add to ketchup and chili.
4. Drain onions, cut in half, and add to the above.
5. Drain tuna well and stir in.
6. When all the ingredients are well combined, spoon into sterilized jars and store in the refrigerator.

*Makes 8 to 9 jars (8 ounces each).*

Hint: *Save the pickle juice and pour over drained canned beets. Store in refrigerator for instant pickled beets!*

## CHEESE WAFERS

*These versatile little "cookies" can be served with cocktails, at a wine-and-cheese party, or with tomato juice, soups, or salads. They also make a welcome gift. Keep them in mind for a deserving grandmother on the next gift-giving occasion.*

**1 package Imperial Cheddar cheese***
**(comes in a flat round red container)**

**½ cup margarine or butter**

**1 cup flour**

**¼ teaspoon chili powder**

**1½ cups bacon chips (not bacon bits)****

Utensils needed

**electric mixer**

**cookie sheet**

1. Turn oven to 350 degrees F.
2. Place cheese and margarine in small bowl of electric mixer and beat until well combined.
3. Gradually beat in flour and chili powder.
4. Gently stir in the bacon chips by hand.
5. Roll into small balls and place on an ungreased cookie sheet. Flatten with a fork (first dip the fork into a glass of cold water).
6. Bake for 10 to 12 to minutes or until the cookies are just beginning to turn a golden brown around the edges.

*Serves 12 to 16.*

* If you are unable to locate Imperial Cheddar, substitute 1 cup grated sharp Cheddar cheese.

** One cup Rice Krispies may be substituted for the ½ cup bacon chips.

# CRAB & CHEESE PLATTER

*You will have a difficult time convincing your guests that you are a complete beginner when you appear with this gorgeous appetizer. It is one of the most attractive dips you will ever see.*

**2 large packages (8 ounces each) cream cheese**

**2 tablespoons lemon juice**

**2 tablespoons Worcestershire sauce**

**2 tablespoons mayonnaise**

**2 tablespoons onion flakes**

**1 large bottle seafood cocktail sauce**

**1 can (6.5 ounces) crabmeat**

**Crackers or vegetables**

Utensils needed

**blender or electric mixer**

**large round platter**

**can opener**

1. Mix together the cream cheese, lemon juice, Worcestershire sauce, mayonnaise, and onion flakes in a blender, or beat with an electric mixer, until smooth and creamy.
2. Spread cheese mixture evenly over the surface of a large round platter, leaving room around the outside for a row of crackers or vegetables.
3. Press the center of the cheese mixture down lightly to make a slightly raised border, about ½ to 1 inch wide, around the outer edge.
4. Spread seafood sauce over the cheese layer within this border so you leave an outside rim of cheese layer showing.

5. Drain the crabmeat. Spread drained crabmeat over the sauce layer, again leaving a border of seafood sauce showing.
6. Serve with crackers or vegetables.

*Serves 10 to 12.*

## SAVORY RITZ BITES

*Have copies of this recipe ready to hand to friends, who will insist you share it. Make sure you buy the right Mini Ritz Bites (cheese-filled, not peanut butter–filled). Be forewarned: These are as addictive as peanuts!*

**½ cup canola oil**

**1 package Hidden Valley Ranch Salad Dressing Mix (the original)**

**1 heaping tablespoon dillweed**

**1 teaspoon garlic powder**

**1 teaspoon celery salt**

**2 boxes Mini Ritz Bites with Cheese**

Utensils needed

**small bowl**

**large plastic container with a tight-fitting lid**

1. Combine oil, dressing mix, dillweed, garlic powder, and celery salt in a small bowl and stir well.
2. Empty Mini Ritz Bites into a large plastic container with a tight-fitting lid.
3. Stir oil-seasoning mixture again to mix well and pour over top of Ritz Bites.
4. Shake gently to distribute seasoned oil evenly.
5. Store in refrigerator for at least 24 hours, turning container upside down several times to mix thoroughly.

*Serves 20 to 24.*

# MEXICAN PIE PLATE DIP

**1 package (8 ounces) cream cheese, room temperature**

**1 cup salsa**

**1 cup grated Cheddar, Monterey Jack, or mozzarella cheese**

**1 package (8 ounces) tortilla chips**

Utensils needed

**grater**

**9-inch glass pie plate**

1. Turn oven to 325 degrees F.
2. Spread cream cheese in bottom of a 9-inch glass pie plate.
3. Spread salsa over top of cream cheese.
4. Top with grated cheese.
5. Bake for 10 to 15 minutes or until cheese is melted.
6. Serve with tortilla chips for dipping.

*Serves 8 to 10.*

## CRANBERRY & FETA PINWHEELS

**1 package (170 grams) sweetened dried cranberries**

**1 container (8-ounce round plastic container) spreadable cream cheese**

**1 cup crumbled feta or grated Cheddar cheese**

**¼ cup chopped green onions**

**3 large flour tortillas (spinach, whole wheat, or plain)**

Utensils needed

**small bowl**

**plastic wrap**

1. Put all of the ingredients except the tortillas in a small bowl and mix well.
2. Divide and spread mixture evenly over tortillas.
3. Roll up tightly (jelly roll style), wrap in plastic wrap, and refrigerate for at least 1 hour.
4. To serve, cut into 12 slices.

*Makes 48 slices.*

Note: *These also can be served hot. Place in a preheated oven at 400 degrees F just until the cheese melts (this will take only a few minutes).*

# NACHOS (HOT & SIMPLE)

*A popular way to serve these is with sour cream, guacamole, or taco sauce to dip, but they are fine as is. Have lots of napkins on hand.*

**½ pound sharp Cheddar cheese, grated**

**½ pound Monterey Jack cheese, grated**

**4 to 6 jalapeño peppers, seeded and finely chopped***

**½ cup chopped onion**

**Tortilla chips**

Utensils needed

**grater**

**ovenproof platter**

1. Turn oven to 350 degrees F.
2. Mix together the cheeses, peppers, and onion.
3. Spread half the chips on an ovenproof platter. Sprinkle this layer with half the cheese mixture.
4. Spread remaining chips over the cheese layer, then top with remaining cheese.
5. Bake for 15 to 20 minutes or broil until hot and bubbly.

*Serves 8 to 10.*

* These peppers are found in the Mexican food section of the supermarket or in with the specialty vegetables. Wash your hands immediately after seeding and chopping the peppers. If you happen to touch your eyes, it will irritate terribly.

# NACHOS WITH CHEESE DIP

**1 jar (16 ounces) Cheese Whiz**

**1 can (4 ounces) chopped green chilies**

**Tortilla chips**

Utensils needed

**small saucepan or microwave-safe round dish**

**can opener**

1. Empty Cheese Whiz into small saucepan or a microwave-safe dish.
2. Drain chilies and stir into Cheese Whiz.
3. Heat in microwave or on stovetop just until heated through.
4. Serve warm over chips.

*Serves 12 to 16.*

# GUACAMOLE

2 ripe avocados

4 tablespoons sour cream

2 tablespoons mayonnaise

2 teaspoons lemon juice*

1 clove garlic, peeled and minced

1 tablespoon finely chopped green onion

1 teaspoon salt

¼ teaspoon pepper

2 tablespoons chopped green chilies (optional)

Corn or tortilla chips

Utensils needed

mixing bowl

serving dish

1. Mash avocados in bowl and stir in all remaining ingredients.
2. Empty into a serving dish. Serve with corn or tortilla chips.

*Serves 8.*

* Don't leave out the lemon juice. It helps prevent discoloration of the avocado.

## POTATO SKINS

**6 small potatoes**

**¼ cup butter, melted**

**½ cup grated Cheddar cheese**

**½ cup grated mozzarella cheese**

Utensils needed

**grater**

**cookie sheet**

1. Turn oven to 375 degrees F.
2. Scrub potatoes, dry them, and bake until soft (about 40 to 45 minutes).
3. Cut potatoes in half lengthwise and scoop out pulp, leaving shell ¼-inch thick.
4. Brush with melted butter and place on cookie sheet.
5. Bake for 5 to 7 minutes, then sprinkle cheeses over buttered skins and return to oven for an additional 5 to 7 minutes.

*Serves 6.*

*Suggested Accompaniment:* Serve hot with sour cream, chopped green onions, and finely crumbled cooked bacon.

# TACO DIP

*Our friend Karen makes this popular dip, which definitely has a "South of the Border" flavor when you add 1 can (4 ounces) of diced green chilis. This is especially popular with teenagers.*

**1 pound lean ground beef**

**½ cup chopped onion**

**1 can tomatoes, chopped and drained**

**1 pound Velveeta cheese (cubed)**

**Corn or tortilla chips**

Utensils needed

**large frying pan**

**medium-size, microwave-safe dish**

1. Sauté ground beef in a large frying pan until browned.
2. Stir in onion and cook until soft.
3. Stir in tomatoes and cheese.
4. Remove from heat and transfer mixture to a medium-size, microwave-safe dish.
5. Cover and microwave on high until cheese is melted.
6. Serve hot with corn or tortilla chips

*Serves 8 to 10.*

## CREAM CHEESE TOPPINGS

*If you like to entertain–sometimes on the spur of the moment–never be without a block of cream cheese in the refrigerator and a package of Carr's Water Crackers on the shelf. Here are just a few things you can do with these ingredients.*

*Variations:*

1. Cover top with jalapeño pepper jelly. Serve on a plate surrounded by crackers and accompanied by a small spreading knife.
2. Spread top with chutney and serve as in #1.
3. Poke holes in cream cheese with a skewer; pour soy sauce over top. This should then sit all day. Just before serving, sprinkle toasted sesame seeds all over top. (Toasted sesame seeds are available in the Chinese section of the supermarket. And while you are there, pick up a package of Chinese rice crackers to serve with this dip.)
4. Spread A-1 Steak Sauce over the top and serve as in #1.

## SPINACH DIP IN HOLLOWED-OUT LOAF

*Very impressive—and it's hearty, healthy, and in an edible bowl. Hooray! No dish to wash!*

**1 round loaf of sourdough or pumpernickel bread (oval would do as well)**

**1 package (10 ounces) frozen spinach, well defrosted, drained, and chopped**

**1 cup mayonnaise**

**1 cup sour cream**

**1 large red onion, finely chopped**

**1 can (10 ounces) water chestnuts, drained and chopped**

**1 package Hickory Farms Red Onion Dip, or any dehydrated vegetable dip of your choice**

Utensils needed

**serrated-edged knife**

**can opener**

**large serving platter**

1. Using a serrated-edged knife (bread knife), cut a circle out of the top of the loaf, leaving a 1-inch edge all around the circumference.
2. Hollow out loaf and cut insides (and top of loaf) into 1-inch cubes (to be used for dipping purposes).
3. Mix remaining ingredients together and spoon into hollowed-out loaf.
4. Serve on a large platter surrounded by the bread cubes.
5. Have a basket of crudites (fresh vegetables cut into finger-size pieces) or extra crackers on hand. They'll love it!

*Serves 10 to 12.*

# HUMMUS WITH TOASTED PITA TRIANGLES

- **1 can (19 ounces) garbanzo beans (chickpeas)**
- **½ cup juice, saved from draining the garbanzo beans**
- **½ cup sesame seeds**
- **2 cloves garlic, minced**
- **2 tablespoons fresh lemon juice**
- **¾ teaspoon salt**
- **Pita bread or Toasted Pita Triangles**

Utensils needed

- **can opener**
- **blender**

1. Drain the garbanzo beans, saving ½ cup juice.
2. Place the sesame seeds and the juice saved from the beans into a blender, and blend on high speed until well blended.
3. Add the beans, garlic, lemon juice, and salt and blend again until smooth.
4. Serve chilled or at room temperature surrounded by plain pita bread or Toasted Pita Triangles.

Note: *Serve a little dish of Greek olives on the side to nibble on as well!*

## Toasted Pita Triangles

**1 package pita bread**

**Olive oil (roughly ⅓ to ½ cup) or nonstick vegetable spray**

Utensils needed

**scissors**

**cookie sheet**

**container with tight lid**

1. Turn oven to 350 degrees F.
2. With a pair of sharp scissors, cut pita bread into triangles and very gently pry apart each triangle (wedge) into two triangles. Brush the rough sides very lightly with olive oil or lightly spray with nonstick vegetable oil.
3. Place pita triangles in a single layer on a cookie sheet and bake for about 5 minutes or until crisp.
4. Let cool and store in a tightly covered container.

*Serves 8 to 10.*

# BAKED WHOLE GARLIC

**4 whole bulbs (heads) garlic**

**⅛ teaspoon salt**

**⅛ teaspoon black pepper (freshly ground is best)**

**¼ cup best-quality olive oil**

**1 small loaf French bread**

Utensils needed

**scissors**

**shallow baking dish or glass pie plate**

**heated plates**

1. Heat oven to 200 degrees F.
2. Remove papery outer skin from the top half of each bulb of garlic to expose the tops of the individual cloves.
3. With scissors, snip the tops off each clove of garlic (the pointed ends). You want to expose the top portion of each clove so that after baking, the soft garlic paste can be easily squeezed from the bulb.
4. Place bulbs in shallow baking dish or glass pie plate and add salt and pepper.
5. Drizzle with olive oil (approximately 1 tablespoon per bulb).
6. Bake, uncovered, for 15 minutes.
7. Cover and continue baking for 1 hour or until garlic is tender, basting occasionally with pan liquid.
8. Serve on heated plates with sliced French bread (guests squeeze the garlic onto the bread and consume with enthusiasm).

*Serves 4 (each person gets to squeeze his or her very own bulb).*

# ENGLISH MUFFIN WEDGES

**1½ cups grated Cheddar cheese**

**½ cup mayonnaise**

**⅓ cup bacon chips (Do not substitute bacon bits, which are smaller and tend to get lost.)**

**8 English muffins, cut in half (into two circles)**

Utensils needed

**grater**

**cookie sheet**

1. Combine grated cheese, mayonnaise, and bacon chips.
2. Spread over cut side of muffins and place muffin halves on a cookie sheet under a preheated broiler for 3 to 5 minutes.
3. Cut in halves or quarters and serve hot.

*Makes 16.*

Note: *You may mix the mayonnaise and cheese ahead of time but do not stir in the bacon chips until just before using, as they tend to get soggy.*

# DAVID'S COCKTAIL ALMONDS

*The just-right salty taste the soy sauce imparts to the skin of these toasty almonds makes them addictive. They are a very welcome house gift, especially if you put them in an attractive reusable container.*

**1 pound unblanched almonds (almonds with skins on)**

**2 tablespoons soy sauce**

Utensils needed

**cookie sheet**

**large bowl**

1. Spread the almonds on a cookie sheet and bake in a preheated oven at 350 degrees F for 18 to 20 minutes. (The almonds should be toasty brown on the inside. Bite into one to check, but be careful not to burn your tongue.)
2. Empty hot almonds into a large bowl and immediately pour the soy sauce over them. They will hiss a bit and smell odd, but start stirring right away and keep stirring until the almonds are well coated and all the soy sauce has been absorbed.
3. Spread the nuts on a cookie sheet and let them dry for about an hour. They can be stored in a covered container for 2 months.

*Serves 12 to 16.*

# BRUSCHETTA

- 4 cups finely chopped fresh tomatoes
- ¼ cup olive oil
- 2 cloves garlic, minced
- ¼ cup grated Parmesan cheese
- 1 to 2 tablespoons Italian seasoning
- 1 loaf French bread or baguette

Utensils needed

- medium-size bowl
- bread knife
- cookie sheet

1. Preheat broiler.
2. In a medium-size bowl, combine tomatoes, oil, garlic, cheese, and seasoning.
3. Cover and place in refrigerator for 2 hours (or overnight).
4. At serving time, slice bread lengthwise and place upside down (cut surface down) on an ungreased cookie sheet.
5. Broil until lightly toasted.
6. Remove from oven; spread surfaces with tomato mixture.
7. Return to broiler and broil 3 to 5 minutes.
8. Remove from oven and slice into serving pieces. Serve hot.

*Serves 8 to 10.*

## HOT ARTICHOKE DIP

*This is perfect for a cocktail party. The men will be "hanging out" around this dish.*

**1 can cream of chicken soup**

**2 packages (8 ounces each) softened cream cheese**

**1 can artichoke hearts, rinsed, drained, and chopped**

**1 can (4 ounces) chopped green chilies**

**½ cup grated Parmesan cheese**

**Paprika**

Utensils needed

**can opener**

**1-quart casserole dish (microwave-safe if using following microwave method)**

1. Turn oven to 375 degrees F.
2. Empty soup and cream cheese in a 1-quart casserole dish and stir until as smooth as possible.
3. Stir in artichokes, chilies, and Parmesan cheese.
4. Bake for 15 minutes or until hot and bubbling.
5. Stir, then sprinkle with paprika.

*Suggested Accompaniments:* Serve hot with bagels cut into bite-size pieces for dippers or with your favorite crackers.

## To Microwave

Stir soup and cheese together in a 1½-quart microwave-safe casserole dish until smooth. Stir in artichokes, chilies, and Parmesan cheese. Microwave uncovered on high for 6 minutes or until hot, stirring twice during cooking.

*Makes 3½ cups.*

Note: *A smaller similar lowfat version of this dish can be made by placing the drained can of artichokes in a food processor with 1 cup light mayonnaise and ¾ cup grated Parmesan cheese. Process until fairly smooth. If desired, a can of chilies can be stirred in at this time or they can be omitted. Pour into a small oven-proof casserole dish and bake at 350 degrees F for 10 to 12 minutes or until bubbly. Serve hot. Makes roughly 2 cups.*

# Soups & Sandwiches

## Soups

Soup Combinations
Minestrone Soup
Instant Borscht with Beef
Chicken Bone Soup
Quick Clam Chowder
Corn Chowder
French Onion Soup
Lasagne Soup

## Sandwiches

Sandwich Combinations
Broiled Tuna on a Bun
Zesty Wieners
Individual Pizzas
Reuben Sandwiches
Ham & Cheese—Hot or Cold
Easy Egg Salad

### Helpful Hint

If too much salt has been added to soups or stews, add a potato. It will absorb the salt.

# SOUP COMBINATIONS

*There are some excellent soup mergers, resulting in flavors unlike the canned soups with which people are familiar, so they taste like homemade. We will list our favorite combinations.*

1. Combine 1 can of tomato soup with 1 can of onion soup, ¼ teaspoon of garlic powder, and 1½ cans of water. Heat. Serve garnished with dabs of sour cream.

2. Combine 1 can of tomato soup, 1 can of pea soup, 1 can of water, 1 cup of milk, and ⅛ teaspoon curry powder. Heat and serve.

3. Combine 1 can of cream of chicken soup and 1 can of potato soup with 1½ cups of milk and ½ cup of sour cream in a blender to create a very easy and palatable vichyssoise. (Vichyssoise is a cold potato soup.)

4. Combine 1 can of consommé and 1 can of tomato soup plus 1 can of water to produce a nice tomato bouillon. Heat and serve. Garnish with chopped fresh parsley.

5. Combine 1 can of onion soup with ¾ cup of whipping cream, sprinkle with Parmesan cheese, and call it "Onion Velvet." Heat and serve.

6. If you want to make French Onion Soup in a hurry, combine 1 can of onion soup with ¾ cup of water and 1 tablespoon of either red or white wine. Sprinkle with garlic croutons, grated Swiss cheese, and Parmesan cheese, in that order, and place under the broiler until cheese is golden and bubbly.

7. Combine 1 can of Cheddar cheese soup, ½ cup of whipping cream, and ¼ can of flat beer; heat. Garnish with bacon bits or chopped celery.

8. We even have a suggestion for a soup using vegetable juice! Heat V-8 juice; place 1 tablespoon of cooked and crumbled bacon in the bottom of each dish, then add the hot juice and top with 1 tablespoon of Parmesan cheese. Great!

9. Combine 1 can cream of mushroom soup, 1 can cream of asparagus soup, and 1 can crabmeat, drained, with 2 cups cereal cream (half-and-half) and ¼ cup sherry. Heat and serve.

# MINESTRONE SOUP

*For your first homemade, hearty, stick-to-the-ribs soup, try this with some crusty French (or Italian) bread. A great treat for lunch or supper on a cold day. This may be made a day or two ahead and kept in the refrigerator; it also freezes well.*

**1½ pounds lean ground beef**

**1 medium onion**

**1 rib celery**

**1 large can (28 ounces) tomatoes**

**2 cans (10 ounces each) onion soup**

**5 cups water**

**2 tablespoons chopped fresh parsley**

**½ teaspoon thyme**

**¼ teaspoon oregano**

**¼ teaspoon sweet basil**

**¼ teaspoon black pepper**

**¾ teaspoon salt**

**½ teaspoon sugar**

**1 package (1 pound) frozen mixed vegetables**

**1 jar (14 ounces) of your favorite spaghetti sauce**

**½ cup broken uncooked spaghetti, about 2 inches in length**

**Grated Parmesan cheese**

Utensils needed

**large stew pot or Dutch oven**

**chopping knife**

**can opener**

1. Cook ground beef over medium heat in a large stew pot or Dutch oven until crumbly, then drain off accumulated fat.*
2. Chop the onion and celery.
3. If the canned tomatoes are whole, cut them into bite-size pieces.
4. Add this mixture and all remaining ingredients except frozen vegetables, spaghetti sauce, and spaghetti pieces to meat.
5. Bring to a boil.
6. When mixture has reached a full rolling boil, add frozen vegetables. Simmer for 30 minutes *covered.*
7. Add spaghetti sauce and broken spaghetti pieces and continue to cook, *uncovered* this time, for an additional 30 minutes, stirring occasionally.
8. Serve hot.
9. Pass a side dish of grated Parmesan cheese to sprinkle on top.

*Serves 8 to 10.*

* If you have a microwave oven, put the raw, crumbled ground beef in a plastic colander and place the colander in the microwave on a plate. The plate will catch the fat that will drain off as the meat cooks. Break the meat up with a fork a bit before adding to the soup pot.

# INSTANT BORSCHT WITH BEEF

*A hearty one-dish meal, so tasty and easy to prepare that it's bound to be a favorite. Great accompanied by Whole Wheat Baking Powder Biscuits (see page 28).*

**1 can (19 ounces) sliced or diced beets**

**2 cans (10 ounces each) beef broth**

**1 tablespoon lemon juice**

**1 teaspoon dried dillweed**

**Pinch of garlic powder**

**½ pound lean ground beef**

**6 tablespoons sour cream**

Utensils needed

**can opener**

**blender**

**large saucepan**

1. Whirl undrained beets in the blender until fairly smooth. If you don't have a blender, dice the beets fairly small.
2. Pour beet mixture into a large saucepan.
3. Add beef broth, lemon juice, dillweed, and garlic powder.
4. Bring to a boil over high heat.
5. While soup is heating, form the ground beef into small meatballs by rolling a teaspoonful at a time between the palms of your hands. (Moistening your hands with a bit of cold water will prevent the meat from sticking.)

6. Add meatballs to boiling soup, cover saucepan, and reduce heat. Simmer slowly until meat is cooked through, about 10 minutes.
7. Serve in individual soup bowls with a dollop of sour cream. Sprinkle the sour cream with a dash of dillweed for flair.

*Serves 6.*

# CHICKEN BONE SOUP

*A good cook is also a thrifty one, and no self-respecting budget-wise gourmet cook would be caught throwing away perfectly good chicken or turkey bones.*

**Leftover chicken carcass**

**1 large onion, cut in chunks**

**3 stalks celery, cut in chunks**

**4 sprigs fresh parsley**

**1 bay leaf**

**½ teaspoon thyme**

**4 carrots, diced**

**3 stalks celery, diced**

**4 potatoes, diced**

**Any leftover chicken meat**

**Salt and pepper**

Utensils needed

**Dutch oven or soup pot (6 quarts)**

**strainer**

**large bowl**

1. Place chicken bones in the Dutch oven or soup pot and cover with cold water.
2. Add onion and celery chunks, parsley, bay leaf, and thyme.
3. Bring to a boil over high heat, then reduce heat and simmer, partially covered, for 3 to 4 hours.

4. Check continually that vegetables and bones remain covered with water. You may need to add water several times during this cooking period.
5. Following cooking time, strain the soup stock into a large bowl. Discard the vegetables and bones but save any pieces of chicken meat and add to the strained broth.
6. Transfer broth back to the original soup pot. Add diced carrots, celery, potatoes, and any leftover chicken meat.
7. Season to taste with salt and pepper.
8. Simmer gently until vegetables are tender, about 30 minutes.

*Serves 6 to 8.*

*Variation:* You may prefer to add ½ cup uncooked rice or 1 cup uncooked fine noodles instead of potatoes. And if you can't get fresh parsley, use 1 tablespoon dried parsley flakes.

# QUICK CLAM CHOWDER

*This delicious, hearty chowder comes from a friend who would rather be out duck hunting than cooking, so you know it'll be fast to fix as well as satisfying.*

**4 strips bacon**

**1 medium onion**

**1 can (10 ounces) New England clam chowder**

**1 can (10 ounces) cream of potato soup**

**1 can (10 ounces) cream of celery soup**

**2 soup cans of milk**

**1 can (5 ounces) baby clams**

**Salt and pepper**

Utensils needed

**chopping knife**

**small frying pan**

**large saucepan**

**can opener**

1. Cut the bacon into ¼-inch strips and fry over medium heat until cooked but not crisp.
2. Dice the onion into small pieces and add to bacon.
3. Fry gently until onion becomes transparent.
4. In a large saucepan, combine the soups and milk. Warm over low heat.
5. Add bacon, onions, and clams and, over low temperature, simmer for 10 to 15 minutes.
6. Season with salt and pepper to taste at serving time. Garnish with freshly chopped parsley or oyster crackers (optional).

*Serves 6 to 8.*

## CORN CHOWDER

**3 slices bacon**

**1 tablespoon butter**

**¼ cup chopped onion**

**¼ cup chopped green pepper**

**1 can (10 ounces) cream of potato soup**

**1 can (14 ounces) cream-style corn**

**1 soup can of milk**

**2 tablespoons chopped pimiento (optional)**

**Salt and pepper**

Utensils needed

**chopping knife**

**small frying pan**

**large saucepan**

**can opener**

1. Cut bacon into ½-inch pieces.
2. Fry bacon until crispy and drain off fat.
3. Melt the butter in the saucepan and add onion and green pepper. Cook over low heat until vegetables are soft, about 5 minutes.
4. Add the undiluted potato soup, corn, and milk. Stir until well blended and cook over medium heat until soup is well heated through.
5. Stir in bacon and pimiento and season with salt and pepper to taste.

*Serves 2 to 3.*

Note: *To serve more people, simply double the quantities.*

# FRENCH ONION SOUP

*Restaurateurs tell us this is still their most-requested soup. It is fun and not too difficult to make at home, but you must have the proper bowls.*

**2 medium onions**

**2 tablespoons oil**

**2 tablespoons butter**

**1 tablespoon flour**

**2 cans (10 ounces each) beef bouillon**

**2 soup cans of water**

**2 tablespoons tomato paste***

**½ teaspoon paprika**

**¼ teaspoon salt**

**4 thin rounds French bread****

**½ cup grated mozzarella cheese*****

**¼ cup grated Swiss Gruyère cheese**

**¼ cup grated Parmesan cheese**

* If you have no tomato paste, use 1 tablespoon tomato ketchup. If you open a fresh can of tomato paste and have no immediate use for the remainder, measure the paste into 1-tablespoon lots on plastic wrap and wrap tightly into small individual packets. Freeze until needed. So many recipes call for 1 or 2 tablespoons of tomato paste; these are very useful to have on hand.

** Instead of French bread, you may slice French rolls. In a pinch, you may substitute packaged croutons–1 to 2 tablespoons per bowl.

*** You may want to use all Swiss cheese instead of part mozzarella. The taste will be good, but we find combining the two cheeses gives the right degree of "stringiness."

Utensils needed

**sharp knife**

**large saucepan or Dutch oven**

**can opener**

**wooden spoon**

**4 ovenproof soup bowls**

1. Slice onions into thin rounds.
2. On top of the stove, slowly heat oil and butter in the saucepan or Dutch oven. Add sliced onions.
3. Cover saucepan and cook the onions very slowly until they are a rich brown color. This will take about 15 minutes. Stir only occasionally at first, but once the onions start to brown, watch them carefully and stir frequently so they do not burn.
4. Stir in the flour. When it has been absorbed, slowly add the bouillon, water, tomato paste, paprika, and salt.
5. Cover and simmer *slowly* for 30 minutes.
6. Toast the French bread slices. (They must be thin or bread will absorb too much of the broth.)
7. Ladle soup into ovenproof bowls.
8. Place a piece of toasted French bread on top of each and cover generously with a mixture of grated mozzarella and Swiss cheese.
9. Sprinkle with the Parmesan cheese and place under the broiler until cheese is brown and bubbly. For easy removal of the bowls from the oven, set them on a baking pan before placing under broiler.
10. Serve immediately.

*Serves 4.*

## LASAGNE SOUP

*Easy to make and even easier to eat. It's not often you can make a soul-satisfying soup like this so quickly.*

- 1 tablespoon olive oil
- 1 pound lean ground beef
- ½ cup chopped onion
- ½ teaspoon salt
- ½ teaspoon black pepper
- 5 cups water
- 1 can (14 ounces) chopped tomatoes, undrained
- 1 can (10 or 12 ounces) whole kernel corn, undrained
- 2 tablespoons grated Parmesan cheese
- 1 package Hamburger Helper Lasagna Mix (you will use the whole box)
- 1 small zucchini, diced

Utensils needed

- Dutch oven or soup pot
- can opener

1. Heat olive oil in bottom of Dutch oven or soup pot.
2. Add ground beef and onion, sprinkle with salt and pepper, and cook over medium heat until meat is no longer pink, separating meat and stirring slightly as it cooks.
3. Add water, tomatoes, corn, Parmesan cheese, and the contents of the sauce mix from the Hamburger Helper Lasagna Mix.
4. Stir until mixed, then bring to a boil over high heat.

5. As soon as soup comes to a boil, cover, then reduce heat to low and simmer for 10 minutes, stirring occasionally.
6. Add the dry noodles from the dinner mix plus the zucchini and continue to simmer, covered, for an additional 10 minutes or until the noodles are tender.

*Serves 6 to 8.*

Note: *This soup thickens when it sits overnight. When reheating leftover soup, add a cup of chicken stock (1 teaspoon of the dry chicken broth mix stirred into 1 cup of boiling water).*

## SANDWICH COMBINATIONS

*We will list a few of our favorite sandwich combinations. The fillings may be put between slices of toasted or plain bread.*

Cold

1. Sliced avocado, crisp bacon, alfalfa sprouts, and mayonnaise. This is best on whole wheat bread.
2. Ham, Swiss cheese, and sliced pickle.
3. Salami, cheese, and very thinly sliced raw mild onion.
4. Sliced cold chicken, tomato, crumbled blue cheese, and mayonnaise.
5. Peanut butter, crumbled crisp bacon, chopped celery, and raisins or peanut butter and lettuce. (Yes, really!)
6. Liverwurst, sliced English cucumber, and sliced raw onion. This is excellent on rye bread.
7. Last and easiest we call our B.C.L.T.: lettuce, sliced tomato, and mayonnaise with bacon chips sprinkled on top.

Hot

1. Grilled cheese: Butter the *outside* of slices of bread, put sliced cheese between the unbuttered sides, and fry over medium heat in a skillet until golden brown on both sides. Peanut butter sandwiches are nice grilled as well.
2. "Christmas Special": Sliced turkey (or chicken), layer of cold stuffing, topped with cranberry sauce, and grilled as in #1.
3. Pepperoni, sliced tomato, sliced raw onion, and a slice of cheese on top placed open-face under the broiler until cheese is melted. Rye bread is best for this.
4. Kelly's Special Open-Faced: Spread a piece of toast with mustard, top this with lightly fried shaved ham, fried chopped onion, and then a fried egg. Serve ketchup on the side. This may be put between two pieces of toast; if so, break the yolk of the egg when you are frying it.

# BROILED TUNA ON A BUN

**1 can (6½ ounces) tuna, drained**

**1½ teaspoons prepared mustard**

**¼ teaspoon Worcestershire sauce**

**¼ cup mayonnaise**

**1½ teaspoons grated onion**

**2 tablespoons chopped green pepper**

**3 hamburger buns, split**

**6 slices tomato**

**½ cup mayonnaise**

**¼ cup grated sharp Cheddar cheese**

Utensils needed

**grater**

**can opener**

**small bowl**

**cookie sheet**

1. Combine first six ingredients in a small bowl.
2. Turn broiler on.
3. Divide tuna mixture equally between the six hamburger bun halves.
4. Top the tuna mixture with a slice of tomato.
5. Combine mayonnaise and shredded cheese and spread on slices of tomato.
6. Place buns on a cookie sheet and, with oven door open, broil about 4 inches away from heat until tops are golden brown; they will puff up slightly.

*Serves 6.*

*Variation:* If you want to fuss a bit, combine the first six ingredients and, using a package of refrigerator biscuits, proceed as follows:

1. Turn oven to 375 degrees F.
2. Separate the biscuits; there will be 10.
3. Roll biscuits into the shape of flat pancakes on a lightly floured surface.
4. Spoon tuna mixture equally onto five of these pancakes.
5. Top with remaining circles and seal by pressing around the edges with a fork.
6. Place on an ungreased baking sheet and bake in heated oven for 15 minutes or until browned.
7. Serve warm or cold. These freeze well.

## ZESTY WIENERS

*This is perfect TV-watching food. It is easy to make and so tasty.*

**Per person:**

**Butter for greasing**

**1 slice of white bread**

**2 good-quality wieners, uncooked**

**1 tablespoon mayonnaise**

**1 tablespoon ketchup**

**1 tablespoon mustard**

Utensils needed

**cookie sheet**

**small bowl or cup**

1. Grease the cookie sheet.
2. Turn oven to 350 degrees F.
3. Lay the slice of bread on the greased cookie sheet.
4. Split wieners lengthwise and lay flat on top of bread.
5. Mix remaining ingredients in the bowl and spread on top of wieners.
6. Bake uncovered for 15 minutes.

*Serves 1.*

*Serving Suggestion:* This could be served for supper as well by adding a Tossed Green Salad (see page 91) and a vegetable such as corn or peas to round out the meal.

# INDIVIDUAL PIZZAS

*These are very flexible and a good way to use up bits and pieces in the refrigerator, such as mushrooms, cheese, ham, tomatoes, and olives. Slice whatever you have on hand and place on top of the pizza spread, then put the mozzarella cheese on last.*

**1 jar or can (7¾ ounces) pizza sauce or spread**

**1 package English muffins, split**

**½ cup grated Parmesan cheese**

**Oregano**

**1 package (6 ounces) mozzarella cheese slices**

Utensils needed

**cookie sheet**

1. Turn oven to 450 degrees F.
2. Spread sauce on split side of English muffins on a cookie sheet. The muffins may be toasted or plain, and any unused muffins may be saved in the freezer for an "encore."
3. Sprinkle sauce with Parmesan cheese and a pinch of oregano.
4. Top with a slice of mozzarella cheese—just a bit smaller than the muffin because the cheese will spread a bit when it melts.
5. Bake at 450 degrees for 10 to 12 minutes.

*Makes 16.*

*Variation:* You may make a quantity of these for an hors d'oeuvre by using a loaf of party rye bread and following the above instructions.

## REUBEN SANDWICHES

*These tasty sandwiches are great to serve to the gang as a late-night snack. You may make them up ahead of time and pop them into the oven just before serving. Don't forget the dill pickles.*

**Butter**

**12 slices rye bread**

**Mustard (Dijon or a good hot variety)**

**12 thin slices lean corned beef**

**¾ cup sauerkraut, drained**

**6 slices mozzarella cheese**

Utensils needed

**knife**

**aluminum foil**

1. Turn oven to 400 degrees F.
2. Butter the bread, and spread mustard sparingly on half the bread slices.
3. Put a slice of corned beef on top of the mustard. (You may prefer to use more corned beef.)
4. Spread about 2 tablespoons of sauerkraut evenly on top of corned beef on each sandwich.
5. Top with a cheese slice, the remaining corned beef slices, and then the other piece of bread.
6. Wrap sandwiches individually in foil.
7. Bake for 20 to 30 minutes at 400 degrees F.

*Serves 6.*

*Variation:* These also are good done on top of the stove in a frying pan. Instead of wrapping the sandwiches in foil, butter the outsides and heat in the frying pan until the outside is toasted and cheese has melted inside.

## HAM & CHEESE—HOT OR COLD

*Hot is more popular because just the idea of cheese melting over succulent ham seems to trigger the salivary glands.*

Hot

**Per person:**

**1 crusty French roll**

**Butter**

**1 tablespoon Thousand Island dressing**

**1 thin slice of ham**

**1 slice of Swiss cheese***

Utensils needed

**bread knife**

**aluminum foil**

1. Turn oven to 350 degrees F.
2. Slice roll in half.
3. Butter halves lightly, then spread with Thousand Island dressing.
4. Place 1 slice of ham on the bottom half of the roll and cover this with a slice of cheese.
5. Wrap bun in aluminum foil.
6. Place in oven at 350 degrees for 10 minutes.

*Serves 1.*

Cold

*Ingredients are the same as above but, since it is not going to be baked, add crisp lettuce. Russian dressing may be substituted for the Thousand Island.*

* Dofino Havarti cheese is nice as well.

# EASY EGG SALAD

**Per person:**

**1 hard-boiled egg (see page 2)**

**2 teaspoons Miracle Whip**

**Sprinkle of salt**

**Sprinkle of pepper**

**2 slices bread, buttered**

Utensils needed

**small bowl**

1. Remove shell from egg. (Grasp the egg in one hand and softly tap it all over with the back of a spoon. Gently strip the shell away from the white of the egg, peeling off the clinging membrane at the same time. You may want to rinse the egg under cold water to make sure there are no remaining shell fragments.)
2. In a small bowl, mash the egg with a fork. When well mashed, stir in the Miracle Whip. (You may want to add more or less than we have recommended depending on how moist or dry you like your egg salad sandwich.)
3. Sprinkle with salt and pepper and spread between two slices of buttered bread.

*Serves 1.*

*Variation:* A bit of chopped green onion makes a good addition to this filling.

Note: *This filling may not be frozen.*

# Salads

# TOSSED GREEN SALAD

*The star of this salad is most often the dressing, but it must also feature* fresh, *unblemished lettuce. Choose from the following. (Supermarkets usually have the names, plus the price, above each variety of lettuce so you can identify them.)*

**Boston (or Bibb)**

**Romaine**

**Curly Endive**

**Iceberg**

**Leaf (all green or with red around the edges, called Red Leaf)**

## Helpful Hints

1. To ripen avocados, tomatoes, or any fruit, place in a brown paper bag or under a plastic dome with a ripe apple. The apple gives off a gas that hastens the ripening of the fruit. When fruit is ripe, store in the refrigerator.
2. Don't add salad dressing to salad until the last minute because the oil causes lettuce to wilt.
3. Don't throw out your leftover salad! Put it in a blender or food processor with 1 cup of tomato or V-8 juice, then blend until smooth for a tasty, economical, and nutritious soup. Serve hot or cold.
4. To unmold: Run a hot knife around the edge of the mold. Place a chilled serving dish over the top of the mold, then turn it upside down. The molded salad should come out easily, but if it doesn't, dip the bottom of the mold into hot water very briefly, then repeat the original procedure.

Utensils needed

**plastic bags**

**salad bowl**

1. Separate leaves. Wash lettuce thoroughly.
2. Dry. (If you have a spinner, so much the better; if not, use paper towels.)
3. Store in plastic bags in the refrigerator until ready to use.
4. At serving time, break lettuce into bite-size pieces into the salad bowl.
5. Add dressing.*

*Serves 4.*

*Variation:* If it is to be for a party, use a combination of different kinds of lettuce, and add one or two (or all) of these suggested additions:

Croutons

Wedges of tomato

Sliced avocado

Crisp bacon bits

Sliced raw mushrooms

Cubed Swiss cheese

Sliced cucumber

Radishes

Small raw broccoli florets

Very thin slices of mild onion, separated into rings

* See the following recipe for Favorite Salad Dressing.

## FAVORITE SALAD DRESSING

**½ cup oil**

**2 tablespoons lemon juice***

**½ teaspoon salt**

**¼ teaspoon black pepper**

**½ teaspoon Worcestershire sauce**

**½ teaspoon prepared mustard**

**⅛ teaspoon garlic powder**

**1 tablespoon grated Parmesan cheese**

Utensils needed

**jar with lid**

1. Place all ingredients in a jar and shake well.
2. Shake again just before adding to salad.

*Makes ¾ cup.*

* You may prefer to substitute wine vinegar (red, white, or balsamic) for the lemon juice.

## CAESAR SALAD

*Beginners should not try to cope with making this at the table, which is traditional. Making the dressing ahead and tossing the salad in the kitchen just before serving will make things less confusing.*

**1 large head of Romaine lettuce**

**1 cup garlic-flavored croutons**

**2 tablespoons grated Parmesan cheese**

Utensils needed

**plastic bag**
**large salad bowl**

1. Early in the day, wash lettuce thoroughly, then dry. (If you have no spinner, paper towels will do—just wrap leaves up and press very gently.)
2. Tear into bite-size pieces and store in a plastic bag in the refrigerator until serving time.
3. When ready to serve, empty lettuce into the salad bowl, shake dressing and pour over lettuce, and toss until lettuce leaves are glossy.
4. Sprinkle croutons and Parmesan cheese on top and toss again, only enough to mix in lightly.

*Serves 4 to 6.*

## Caesar Salad Dressing

- ½ cup olive oil
- 2 tablespoons lemon juice
- 1 teaspoon red wine vinegar
- 1 small clove garlic, minced
- ¼ teaspoon prepared mustard
- ⅛ teaspoon Worcestershire sauce
- 1 egg
- 4 capers
- ½ can anchovies, drained (2 ounces)
- ¼ teaspoon salt

Utensils needed

- blender
- medium bowl
- can opener
- garlic press

1. Put all the ingredients in a blender and blend for about 20 seconds or until creamy. Put in medium bowl and store in refrigerator. This dressing will keep in the refrigerator for about 1 week. (If you don't want to be left with half a can of anchovies, double the recipe. It's so good, you will use it up.)

## MARINATED RAW VEGETABLE SALAD

*Most people know about this salad but maybe not the beginning cook–and he or she definitely should. It is perfect for a buffet. You may vary the assortment of vegetables to suit your taste. The following is just a guide. (Be sure to wash all the vegetables. There might be little "critters" hiding in the broccoli and cauliflower in particular; soak these two vegetables in cold, salted water for about 10 minutes to get rid of any animal life!)*

**1 head cauliflower**

**2 large stalks broccoli**

**2 large carrots**

**1 medium zucchini**

**2 stalks celery**

**1 green pepper**

**1 small bunch radishes**

**¼ pound mushroom caps**

**1 basket cherry tomatoes**

**1 bottle (8 ounces) Italian dressing**

Utensils needed

**vegetable peeler**
**large plastic bowl, with lid**
**large salad bowl and servers**

1. Separate cauliflower into florets.
2. Peel the broccoli stalks with a vegetable peeler and cut into bite-size pieces. Separate florets into bite-size pieces.
3. Peel the carrots

4. Slice carrots, unpeeled zucchini, and celery into finger-size pieces.
5. Cut green pepper into wedges and remove seeds.
6. Trim ends of radishes.
7. Wipe the mushrooms (and trim ends of stalks if there are any). You may substitute 1 can of button mushrooms, drained, if you can't get fresh.
8. Place all the vegetables in a plastic container and pour dressing over. Place a tight-fitting lid on container and store vegetables in refrigerator overnight. Turn container upside down occasionally during this marinating period to distribute the dressing evenly. If you do not have a suitable container, use a double plastic bag.
9. Drain vegetables before placing in a salad bowl to serve.

*Serves 16 to 20.*

*Serving Suggestion:* This may be served as an hors d'oeuvre as well. People are much more aware of "empty calories" than ever before and would prefer to snack on fresh vegetables rather than on something encased in pastry (well, most people!).

# SPINACH SALAD

*This salad is becoming more and more popular, but make sure the spinach you use is nice and fresh.*

**½ pound fresh spinach leaves**

**4 slices well-cooked bacon (crisp)**

**1 hard-cooked egg, chopped (optional)**
**(See recipe for Boiled Eggs on page 2.)**

Utensils needed

**salad bowl**

1. Make dressing and set aside (see following recipe).
2. Trim off and discard any tough stems or bruised spinach leaves.
3. Wash well in cold water (spinach tends to be a bit sandy).
4. Shake off any excess water or pat dry with paper towels.
5. Tear the leaves into bite-size pieces into a salad bowl.
6. When ready to serve (not a minute before!), toss the spinach with ¼ cup of the dressing.
7. Sprinkle with the crumbled bacon. (If you are adding the chopped egg, sprinkle it on top with the bacon.)

*Serves 4.*

Dressing

- ⅓ cup corn oil
- 2 tablespoons apple cider vinegar
- 2 tablespoons orange juice
- 1 tablespoon light soy sauce
- ½ teaspoon dry mustard
- 1 teaspoon white sugar
- ¼ teaspoon salt
- Pinch of black pepper

Utensils needed

- small jar with lid

1. Place all of the ingredients in a jar (with a tight lid) and shake well just before using.

Note: *Any unused portion keeps very well in the refrigerator.*

# AVOCADO STUFFED WITH CRABMEAT

*The avocado is rightly touted as being an almost-perfect food–full of essential vitamins and minerals and delicious as well. A favorite preparation with many is half an avocado filled with a bit of vinaigrette or French dressing. For something a bit more "special" try the following.*

**1 large avocado**

**2 teaspoons lemon juice**

**1 can (6 ounces) crabmeat**

**¼ cup chopped celery**

**⅛ teaspoon celery salt**

**1 cup Thousand Island dressing**

Utensils needed

**sharp knife**

**small bowl**

**salad plate**

1. Slice the avocado lengthwise all the way around and, twisting gently, separate into two halves. Remove the pit.
2. Sprinkle exposed surface of avocado with the lemon juice. This prevents discoloration.
3. In a small bowl, combine crabmeat, celery, celery salt, and ¼ cup of Thousand Island dressing. Stuff this into the cavities of the avocado.
4. Place on a lettuce-lined salad plate. Pour the remainder of the Thousand Island dressing over the top. A few cherry tomatoes and sprigs of parsley liven the plate up nicely.

*Serves 2.*

Note: *The avocado will sit better on the plate if you cut a tiny slice from the very bottom to "flatten" it. And should you ever be left with half an avocado, save the pit to place in the unused half and it will keep very well in the refrigerator.*

*Variations:* You may substitute ¾ cup mayonnaise mixed with ¼ cup of chili sauce for the Thousand Island dressing. Also, you may use any kind of seafood–shrimp, lobster, or salmon. It must be canned or cooked; use a small can or 1 cup.

# QUICK COLESLAW

*Using sauerkraut (which is really shredded cabbage) eliminates the most time-consuming task in making coleslaw: shredding the cabbage. However, if you like the taste of sauerkraut you may be disappointed, for there is not a trace in this salad.*

**1 jar (32 ounces) sauerkraut**

**1 cup sugar**

**1 cup diced green pepper**

**1 cup diced celery**

**1 cup chopped onion**

**1 cup grated carrot**

**⅓ cup oil**

**⅓ cup vinegar**

Utensils needed

**colander**

**grater**

**large bowl (not metal)**

**small saucepan**

1. Drain sauerkraut well by pouring it into a colander and pressing all excess moisture out with the back of a spoon. Remove pimiento and discard.
2. Sprinkle sauerkraut with sugar. Stir, and combine with vegetables in a large bowl.
3. Combine oil and vinegar in a small saucepan. Bring to boil over medium heat and boil uncovered for 1 minute. Cool.

4. Pour over salad vegetables in bowl.
5. Refrigerate covered. This will keep in the refrigerator for up to 3 weeks.

*Serves 6 to 8.*

Note: *If you prefer the creamy-type coleslaw and don't mind shredding the cabbage, simply dilute a cup of your favorite commercial-type mayonnaise with a bit of cereal cream (half-and-half) or milk (about 4 tablespoons) and add 1 teaspoon sugar. Blend together well with a fork. Pour this over a small head of shredded cabbage and toss. You might want to include two or three chopped green onions and one grated carrot.*

# CALIFORNIA SALAD (COBB SALAD)

*This is found in the better restaurants all over California, where it originated, and is becoming increasingly popular all over North America. It is attractive, tasty, nourishing, and a great way to use up leftover chicken. Keep all ingredients separate until you assemble them into an attractive pattern in the bowl.*

**1 cup Vinaigrette Dressing (see recipe on page 106)**

**1 small head of iceberg lettuce**

**2 tablespoons chopped chives**

**1 large tomato**

**1 avocado**

**Lemon juice**

**2 hard-boiled eggs**

**8 slices bacon**

**3 ounces blue cheese**

**1½ cups diced, cooked chicken**

Utensils needed

**large, wide salad bowl**

**chopping knife**

**large frying pan**

**jar with lid**

1. Make the following vinaigrette dressing and set aside. The dressing may be made ahead of time and refrigerated.
2. Shred lettuce and place in the bottom of a large, wide salad bowl.
3. Sprinkle lettuce with chives.

4. Cut the tomato in quarters, remove seeds (little finger does it best), then chop the tomato into small pieces. Set aside.
5. Peel and dice the avocado. Sprinkle with a bit of lemon juice to prevent discoloration and set aside.
6. Chop the hard-boiled eggs and set aside.
7. Cook the bacon in the frying pan until crisp. When cool, crumble the bacon with your fingers; set aside.
8. Crumble the cheese and set aside.
9. Now comes the assembly. Shake vinaigrette dressing in a jar with a lid, pour over lettuce and chives, and toss.
10. On top of lettuce and chives, arrange all the other ingredients (including the diced chicken) in separate wedge-shaped sections–like a pinwheel. The cheese usually sits right in the middle, as the hub, rather than having a wedge of its own.
11. Bring to the table and toss again.

*Serves 3 to 4.*

Note: *You may wish to substitute chopped green onion for the chives and diced Cheddar for the blue cheese.*

## Vinaigrette Dressing

**½ cup oil**

**2 tablespoons white wine vinegar**

**½ teaspoon salt**

**¼ teaspoon black pepper**

**⅛ teaspoon garlic powder**

**½ teaspoon Worcestershire sauce**

**Pinch of dry mustard powder**

1. Combine all ingredients in a jar and shake. Shake again just before using.

Note: *Use freshly ground black pepper if you can. It has its own special flavor for salad dressings.*

# ASIAN COLESLAW

**2 packages (3 ounces each) beef flavored noodle soup with mix (Ramen noodles)**

**2 packages (8.5 ounces each) coleslaw mix***

**1 cup slivered almonds****

**1 cup sunflower seeds**

**6 to 8 green onions, chopped**

**½ cup sugar**

**¾ cup vegetable oil**

**⅓ cup white vinegar**

Utensils needed:

**large salad bowl**

1. Remove flavor packets from soup mix and set aside.
2. Break noodles into small pieces and place in bottom of a large salad bowl.
3. Top noodles with coleslaw mix.
4. Sprinkle with almonds, sunflower seeds, and green onions.
5. Whisk together the contents from flavor packets, sugar, oil, and vinegar and pour over coleslaw. (Do not toss yet.)
6. Cover with plastic wrap and chill for 24 hours.
7. Toss well before serving.

*Serves 8 to 10.*

* Coleslaw mix is generally found in the produce section.

** To toast almonds, spread the nuts onto a shallow greased baking pan and place in a preheated 300-degree oven until they start to turn a golden brown. Start checking in about 10 minutes. Cool before adding to salad.

Notes:

1. *Beef-flavored noodles are best for this recipe, but if you have chicken, pork, or vegetable on hand, they work well too.*
2. *If you don't have 24 hours to chill the salad, you can make it and serve it right away, providing coleslaw mix is well chilled.*

# MARINATED CUCUMBER SALAD

*This just disappears when placed on a buffet table. A good accompaniment to ham or any fish dish.*

**2 medium cucumbers or 1 large English cucumber**

**½ cup vinegar**

**2 tablespoons water**

**¼ teaspoon salt**

**⅛ teaspoon white pepper**

**3 tablespoons sugar**

**3 tablespoons finely chopped fresh parsley**

Utensils needed

**sharp knife**

**serving bowl, preferably glass**

1. Slice unpeeled cucumber as thinly as possible and place in a serving bowl, preferably glass.
2. Combine remaining ingredients and stir until the sugar is dissolved.
3. Pour this dressing over the cucumbers. Refrigerate for 4 hours.
4. Drain slightly just before serving. Don't worry if the cucumbers are wilted; they are supposed to look like that.

*Serves 6 to 8.*

## MARINATED ONIONS

*This is as essential to a roast beef buffet as the preceding cucumber salad is to a seafood buffet. Any leftover portion makes great sandwiches when combined with thinly sliced Cheddar cheese.*

**3 large mild onions**

**1 cup vinegar**

**½ cup sugar**

**1 teaspoon celery seed**

**1 cup sour cream**

Utensils needed

**sharp knife**

**large bowl**

1. Slice the onions into thin rings.
2. Combine vinegar and sugar and stir until sugar is dissolved.
3. Arrange onion rings in a large bowl and pour vinegar–sugar mixture over them. Cover.
4. Let sit overnight or for at least 4 hours.
5. Three hours before serving *drain well,* discarding marinade. Stir celery seed into sour cream and toss with onions.

*Serves 8 to 10.*

*Variation:* One-half cup mayonnaise may be substituted for the 1 cup sour cream. Proceed as above.

## FAVORITE CUCUMBER MOLD

*Recipes abound for rich Jell-O molds that are definitely ladies' luncheon fare and seem to be enjoyed mostly by women. So when you are given a recipe by a friend who tells you it is her husband's favorite, don't hesitate to make it for the family or friends. We didn't hesitate and they all loved it. Thank you, Glenn and Sharon!*

**1 small package lemon Jell-O**

**½ cup boiling water**

**2 tablespoons lemon juice**

**Pinch of salt**

**Pinch of white pepper**

**Oil**

**½ cup shredded cucumber**

**½ cup minced celery**

**1 cup sour cream**

Utensils needed

**medium mixing bowl**

**grater**

**4-cup mold**

1. Dissolve Jell-O in boiling water in a medium mixing bowl, stirring until all the powder is dissolved.
2. Add lemon juice, salt, and pepper.
3. Chill in refrigerator until partially set (barely starts to jiggle), about 30 minutes.
4. Lightly oil the mold.

5. Fold cucumber, celery, and sour cream into the Jell-O and pour into the mold.
6. Return to refrigerator until firmly set, about 4 hours.
7. Unmold onto serving plate.*

*Serves 4 to 6.*

Hint: *If Jell-O "over-gels" before you add the remaining ingredients, you can always return it to liquid form by placing over hot water.*

*Variations:* A small can of drained crushed pineapple makes a nice addition. Add this at the same time you are adding the cucumber and celery. Instead of sour cream, you may use yogurt.

* *To Unmold:* Run a hot knife around the edge of the mold. Place a chilled serving dish over the top of the mold, then turn upside down. The molded salad should come out easily, but if it doesn't, dip the bottom of the mold into hot water very briefly, then repeat procedure.

# JANE'S JELLIED TOMATO SALAD

*This is about as easy as a jellied salad ever gets.*

**1 can (14 ounces) stewed tomatoes**

**2 teaspoons white vinegar**

**1 package raspberry Jell-O (4-serving size)**

Utensils needed

**saucepan**

**bowl or gelatin mold**

1. Empty the canned tomatoes into a saucepan and stir in the vinegar.
2. Heat to boiling, remove from heat, and stir in the raspberry Jell-O until it is dissolved.
3. Empty into a bowl or mold (spray with nonstick vegetable oil spray for easy unmolding), and chill in the refrigerator until set—allowing at least 4 to 6 hours (overnight is fine).
4. Unmold and serve.*

*Serves 6 to 8.*

* *To Unmold:* Run a hot knife around the edge of the mold. Place a chilled serving dish over the top of the mold, then turn upside down. The molded salad should come out easily, but if it doesn't, dip the bottom of the mold into hot water very briefly, then repeat procedure.

## GREEK SALAD

*A must with lamb, but also good with steak or barbecued chicken. Make sure you use a good quality feta cheese and the Greek Kalamata olives. If you get the olives at the deli, ask to try one first. Some are great, others just too salty. If you buy them in a jar, a very reliable brand is Unico. If you like lettuce in your Greek salad, add ½ small head of iceberg lettuce, cut into chunks (but you won't find lettuce in a Greek salad in Greece!).*

**1 small English cucumber (or ½ large one), seeded and cut in bite-size chunks**

**2 tomatoes, cut into chunks**

**1 red onion (or other sweet onion), very thinly sliced**

**1 large firm green pepper, seeded and cut into bite-size squares**

**½ to 1 cup feta cheese, crumbled or cut into small chunks**

**½ cup Greek olives**

Utensils needed

**cutting knife**

**salad bowl**

**jar with tight-fitting lid**

1. Put all the above ingredients into a salad bowl and chill until ready to serve.
2. At serving time, toss with the Greek Salad Dressing.*

*Serves 4.*

* If you don't want to make your own dressing, an excellent dressing on Greek salad is Kraft's Signature Collection Greek with Feta and Oregano Dressing and Marinade. If you use this dressing, add ½ teaspoon oregano to the bottle of dressing and shake before using.

## Greek Salad Dressing

**¾ cup quality extra-virgin olive oil**

**¼ cup red wine vinegar**

**1 teaspoon Dijon mustard**

**½ teaspoon salt**

**¼ teaspoon freshly ground black pepper**

**1 teaspoon oregano**

1. Combine all ingredients in a jar and shake until blended. Will keep, refrigerated, for up to 2 weeks. Add only enough dressing to salad to moisten.

# POTATO SALAD

*Potato salad is one of the staples for barbecues, buffets, and hot summer days. Many people believe the best potato salad is made by using cold potatoes, but they're wrong!*

**5 medium potatoes**

**1 cup chopped celery**

**1 cup chopped green onions**

**4 hard-boiled eggs, diced**

**½ cup Miracle Whip or mayonnaise**

**¼ cup sweet pickle juice**

**1 teaspoon prepared mustard**

**1½ teaspoons salt**

**½ teaspoon pepper**

Utensils needed

**potato peeler**
**large saucepan**
**large metal spoon**
**salad bowl**
**small bowl**

1. Peel the potatoes, then boil in a large saucepan until tender. Drain but leave in pot.
2. While they are still piping hot, simply hit each potato with the back of a large metal spoon; potato will break into small pieces.
3. Combine potatoes with celery, onions, and hard-boiled eggs in the salad bowl.

4. In a small bowl blend mayonnaise, pickle juice, mustard, salt, and pepper.
5. Add to potato mixture and toss lightly.
6. Transfer to serving bowl and chill.
7. Just before serving, garnish with extra sliced hard-boiled eggs if desired.

*Serves 4 to 6.*

# ICEBERG LETTUCE WEDGE WITH BLUE CHEESE DRESSING

**1 head iceberg lettuce**

Utensils needed

**cutting knife**

**paper towels**

1. Cut out core (base) of lettuce with a sharp knife.
2. Discard any wilted outer leaves.
3. With lettuce held upside down, hold under cold running water so that the hole you have just created fills with water.
4. Turn right side up and drain until water stops running out.
5. Wrap in two sheets of paper towel and store in refrigerator until needed.
6. Do this at least 1 hour before needed or up to 1 day ahead. The lettuce will be nice and crisp.
7. Cut into four or six wedges (or one or two, depending on how many you need) and serve topped with Blue Cheese (or Roquefort) Dressing (see next recipe). If you would prefer Thousand Island dressing, good bottled dressings are available.

*Serves 6 to 8.*

## Blue Cheese (or Roquefort) Dressing

*Tori's Mom's Favorite!*

**1½ cups mayonnaise**

**2 tablespoons milk (a little more is okay, but don't make it too thin)**

**½ cup crumbled blue cheese (or Roquefort)**

**½ teaspoon Worcestershire sauce**

**¼ teaspoon salt**

**⅛ teaspoon garlic powder**

**⅛ teaspoon white pepper**

1. Mix all the ingredients together. Do not use a blender, as you want to see tiny pieces of cheese.
2. Store in the refrigerator until needed (will keep for 1 week).*
3. Spoon over lettuce wedges when serving.

*Variation:* Try a spoonful of leftover dressing on top of a baked potato. Yummy!

* This dressing will thicken when stored overnight or longer. If necessary, thin with additional milk (or cream) before using.

# THAI PASTA SALAD

1 pound spaghettini (or spaghetti)

2 tablespoons instant chicken bouillon mix

⅓ cup canola oil

1 tablespoon sesame oil

1 teaspoon crushed dry red pepper

⅓ cup liquid honey

¼ cup chicken stock (or ¼ instant bouillon mix dissolved in ¼ cup hot water)

4 tablespoons soy sauce

¾ cup chopped peanuts (the small Spanish type with skins is a good choice)

½ cup chopped green onions

2 tablespoons sesame seeds

Fresh cilantro leaves (optional)

Utensils needed

large cooking pot

small saucepan

large bowl

1. Break spaghettini into thirds and cook in a large pot (a Dutch oven or spaghetti pot) of boiling water to which you have added the 2 tablespoons instant chicken bouillon mix.
2. Cook approximately 10 to 12 minutes (see instructions on package). You want pasta "*al dente,*" which means slightly resilient when pressed between thumb and forefinger. Drain well.

3. Meanwhile, place canola oil, sesame oil, red pepper, and honey in a small saucepan and heat until honey is dissolved.
4. Remove from heat and add chicken stock and soy sauce to saucepan.
5. Pour over cooked spaghettini in a large bowl and toss lightly to mix. There will be a little liquid sitting in the bottom of the bowl, but it will be absorbed when the salad sits in the refrigerator.
6. Cover and refrigerate overnight or for a minimum of 4 to 6 hours.
7. At serving time, toss with the chopped peanuts and green onions and sprinkle with sesame seeds. Fresh cilantro leaves make a suitable and attractive garnish.

*Serves 8 to 10.*

6

# Meat Dishes

Instant Barbecued Spareribs
Jo's Marinated Pork Tenderloin
Sausage & Rice Casserole
Apple-Glazed Pork Roast
Cabbage Roll Casserole
Busy Day Ham Wellington (with Canned Ham)
Broiled Honeyed Ham Steak
Broiled Lamb Chops
Baked Lamb Chops
Barbecued Butterflied Leg of Lamb
Liver with Onions & Bacon

## Helpful Hints

1. Do not salt meat until ready to cook it. Salt tends to draw out the juices.
2. Your roasts, steaks, and chops will be more tender if they are at room temperature when you start cooking rather than taken right from the refrigerator.
3. When making ground beef patties, add grated zucchini instead of bread crumbs. The patties will have a much better texture and flavor.
4. If you don't plan to make gravy with the meat drippings from a roast, line the roasting pan with foil; this makes cleaning up a lot easier.

# ROAST BEEF WITH GRAVY

*You must use a good cut of beef. Standing rib roast is one of the best and is the cut we suggest. When you are trying to decide how large a roast to buy, allow two servings per rib. The following "cook-ahead" method is the very best method for cooking this roast; it is foolproof. You may cook this in the morning or at noon and forget about it until 30 minutes before you plan to serve it. It would be unthinkable to cook this wonderful cut of meat any way but rare or medium-rare. If you insist on well-done beef, buy a pot roast and follow the recipe on page 133. Follow the recipe for homemade Roast Beef Gravy if you're feeling brave.*

**3-rib standing rib roast (ask for the first 3 ribs)**

**Dry mustard powder**

**Coarse black pepper**

Utensils needed

**shallow roasting pan**

1. Have roast at room temperature. (Four hours out of the refrigerator should do it.)
2. Turn oven to 375 degrees F.
3. Rub meat all over with dry mustard and sprinkle fairly heavily with the black pepper. *No salt.*
4. Place the roast fat side up in a shallow roasting pan.
5. Place in oven only when the oven light has gone off to indicate that oven has reached 375 degrees.
6. Cook for 1 hour.
7. Turn oven off but *do not open the oven door for at least 3 hours.* Leave the roast in the oven until 45 minutes before you plan to serve it (time will depend on whether you want it rare or medium-rare).

8. Turn the oven back on to 375 degrees and leave the roast in for 10 minutes *after* the indicator light goes off for rare and 35 minutes for medium-rare. The first cooking (step #6) should be at least 3 hours before the second, but the first cooking may be in the morning so there is no rushing home to put the roast on!

*Serves 6.*

Note: *This method may be used on any size standing rib roast.*

*Suggested Accompaniments:* Mashed Potatoes, Roast Potatoes, or "instant" roast potatoes (for "cook-ahead": just before turning oven on for the second time, arrange drained canned whole potatoes around the roast, sprinkling potatoes with paprika), Broccoli or Cauliflower and Cheese Sauce, marinated onions, and Yorkshire Pudding.

*Variation—Traditional Method:* If you don't want to use the "cook-ahead" method, we strongly suggest buying a meat thermometer and following its guide. You must let the roast sit for 15 minutes when it comes from the oven before carving to allow the juices to settle. The meat will continue to cook a wee bit from the heat of the roast, so remove it from the oven when the thermometer registers just a little under the required temperature.

This is the most accurate method of determining when the roast is cooked. Should you not have a thermometer, use the following timing as a guide:

1. Prepare the roast as for the cook-ahead method.
2. Preheat the oven to 350 degrees F (at least 10 minutes of preheating required to reach this temperature).
3. Cook the roast at 18 minutes per pound for rare, 22 minutes per pound for medium, and 30 minutes per pound for well-done meat.

*continues*

*continued from page 125*

## Roast Beef Gravy

*The easiest way to make gravy is to use a packaged gravy mix or, if you are really nervous, canned gravy–guaranteed not to lump! However, real homemade gravy is very easy to make.*

**2 tablespoons beef drippings (see step 2 in directions below)**

**2 tablespoons all-purpose flour**

**1 cup water**

**Salt and pepper**

### Utensils needed

**aluminum foil**

1. Remove roast from pan and keep warm with foil over top.
2. Pour off all but 2 tablespoons of the drippings and stir the flour into the reserved drippings in the pan until the flour has been absorbed by the fat.
3. Add water and stir constantly over medium heat on top of the stove until thickened. Add salt and pepper to taste.
4. You may want to add a teaspoon of Kitchen Bouquet for color. This is a browning and seasoning sauce found in the section of the supermarket where you find the ketchup.

*Variation:* If you have no roast drippings, substitute 2 tablespoons of butter, but then use canned beef bouillon instead of water. You may want to use Worcestershire sauce or ketchup to zip it up, 1 teaspoon of either, or both.

# YORKSHIRE PUDDING

*You don't have to be from Merrie Olde Englande to love Yorkshire Pudding with your roast beef. It is very simple to make, the only trick being a hot pan containing equally hot drippings. If your Yorkshire Pudding is to accompany Roast Beef but you have only one oven, remove the cooked roast and cover with foil to keep warm while you bake the pudding.*

**2 or 3 tablespoons fat drippings (see step 2 in directions below)**

**¾ cup plus 2 tablespoons all-purpose flour**

**½ teaspoon salt**

**2 large eggs**

**½ cup milk**

**½ cup water**

Utensils needed

**8-inch square baking pan**

**small bowl**

**whisk or fork**

1. Turn oven to 400 degrees F.
2. Put the fat drippings from the roast into the baking pan and place pan in the hot oven.*
3. Combine all remaining ingredients in a bowl and beat with a wire whisk or fork. Don't worry if mixture is a little lumpy.

* Instead of drippings, you may use equal portions of oil and butter, enough to cover the bottom of the pan. Heat as above but watch carefully because butter burns easily.

4. Remove pan from oven and immediately pour batter into pan.
5. Bake for 30 to 40 minutes. Do not at any time lower the heat. The pudding must be served as soon as it is ready. Don't worry if it falls a bit–it is supposed to.

*Serves 6.*

# BROILED FLANK STEAK

*This has more flavor and "character" than the more expensive steaks such as T-bone and sirloin. It's a lot easier on the pocketbook as well. The flank steak usually weighs around 2 pounds, which is perfect for four people. If there are only two, it makes great sandwiches the next day. This steak, however, must be served rare to medium-rare, as it tends to be a little on the tough side if overdone. If you like well-done steak, you'd better choose a different cut.*

1 flank steak (2 pounds)
3 tablespoons oil
4 tablespoons soy sauce
2 teaspoons brown sugar
¼ teaspoon pepper
¼ teaspoon garlic powder
⅛ teaspoon ginger
*No salt*

Utensils needed

sharp knife
small bowl or measuring cup
9- by 13-inch baking pan

1. Try to remove as much of the membrane from the steak as you can do easily.
2. Score the meat on both sides—this means take a sharp knife and make slashes on the diagonal about quarter-way into the flesh, then do the same in the opposite direction so you have created "diamonds" about 1 inch wide. Turn the steak over and do the same on the opposite side.

3. Combine the remaining ingredients in a small bowl—*no salt*—and pour over meat in the baking pan.
4. Let meat marinate in this for about 3 hours. (It is not necessary to refrigerate during this time.) Remove meat from marinade before broiling, but save marinade to pour over steak when cooked.
5. Turn broiler on for 10 minutes—you want it well preheated. When broiling the steak, leave the oven door open.
6. Broil 3 to 4 inches from heat for 5 minutes on one side and 3 to 4 minutes on the other; it will be medium-rare. Flank steak should not be too rare or too well-done.

*Serves 4.*

*Suggested Accompaniments:* Baked Potatoes, Stir-Fried Broccoli, wedges of lettuce with dressing of your choice.

# EYE OF THE ROUND ROAST

*This is sometimes referred to as a shell-bone roast. It is quite lean, easy to carve, and the timing is accurate. Because this lean cut would be dry if cooked to a well-done state, cooking times are listed for rare and medium-rare only. Choose the Oven Pot Roast (see page 133) if you want well-done beef.*

**3- to 4-pound (1.5 to 2 kilograms) eye of the round roast**

**8-ounce bottle of Italian salad dressing (not lowfat)**

Utensils needed

**small shallow pan or zip-lock bag**

**roast pan**

**slicing knife**

1. Place roast in a roast pan or in a zip-lock baggie and pour salad dressing over top, turning to coat well. Let sit in the refrigerator all day (or overnight–even up to 3 days!). Bring to room temperature before roasting to ensure accurate timing.
2. Preheat oven to 325 degrees F.
3. Bake for 20 minutes per pound for rare and 25 minutes per pound for medium rare.
4. When serving, slice thinly across the grain.

*Serves 6 to 8.*

Notes:

1. *If you don't like figuring out times, here is a formula that works well for a 3- to 4-pound eye of the round roast: Roast for 1 hour at 350 degrees F for rare; roast for 1 hour at 400 degrees F for medium-rare.*

2. *Because the eye of round roast has so little fat, it doesn't yield sufficient drippings for gravy. However, there is nothing wrong with using a packaged beef gravy or Knorr Demi-Glace (follow the directions on the package). See the vegetable section for excellent Roast Potatoes (see page 255). If you have any leftovers, you can use them to make Leftover Roast Beef Casserole (see page 135).*

# OVEN POT ROAST

*An easy main dish, with no browning necessary and no gravy to make; it makes its own great gravy.*

**4- to 5-pound chuck roast***

**1 package (1.5 ounces) dehydrated onion soup mix**

**1 can (10 ounces) cream of mushroom soup**

Utensils needed

**Dutch oven or small roasting pan**

**small bowl**

**can opener**

1. Heat oven to 350 degrees F.
2. Place meat in a Dutch oven or roasting pan. (Meat need not have extra space around it.)
3. Mix dry soup mix and undiluted mushroom soup together and pour over and around the meat. Mixture will be thick.
4. Cover tightly with foil or a lid that fits the pan.
5. Bake for 2½ to 3 hours at 350 degrees.

*Serves 6 to 8.*

*Serving Suggestion:* This may be made into a complete one-dish meal by adding potatoes, carrots, onions, turnips, or parsnips for the last hour of cooking. (You may have to use a larger roasting pan for this.)

* Other suitable cuts of meat include rolled brisket or blade roast. If the meat weighs less than 4 pounds, use only part of the onion soup mix but all of the mushroom soup.

# BUSY DAY STEW

*So easy and tasty. Make it in the morning and be greeted by the pleasant aroma of home cooking when you return later in the day.*

**1 medium onion**

**6 stalks celery (optional)**

**3 medium potatoes**

**6 carrots**

**2 pounds lean stewing beef**

**2 teaspoons salt**

**1 tablespoon sugar**

**3 tablespoons minute tapioca**

**1½ cups tomato juice**

Utensils needed

**chopping knife**
**large, shallow, ovenproof casserole or crock pot**

1. Heat oven to 250 degrees F.
2. Chop the vegetables. Cut the onion into small chunks, the celery into 1-inch pieces, the potatoes into quarters, and the carrots into long strips.
3. Combine all ingredients in a shallow casserole.
4. Cover tightly with lid or foil.
5. Bake for at least 4 hours.
6. Once the stew has been cooked, it can stay in the oven for up to 3 to 4 hours; if you will need to hold it longer, add an extra ½ cup tomato juice.

*Serves 4 to 6.*

Note: *Parsnips and turnips are also good additions to a stew.*

# LEFTOVER ROAST BEEF CASSEROLE

*A friend, after eating this dish for the first time, actually bought a roast beef for the following night's dinner–just so she would have leftovers to make this casserole!*

**3 to 4 cups leftover roast beef, cut into cubes**
**1 can (14 ounces) stewed tomatoes**
**1 package dry onion soup mix**
**1 small can (8 ounces) baked beans**
**1 small can (7½ ounces) tomato sauce**
**1 teaspoon garlic salt**
**½ teaspoon oregano**
**2 medium onions, cut into wedges**
**4 medium carrots, peeled and cut into 1-inch chunks**

Utensils needed

**sharp knife**
**casserole dish**

1. Preheat oven to 350 degrees F.
2. Mix all the ingredients together in a deep casserole dish.
3. Cover dish and bake for 1 hour. If the casserole is a little too soupy at this stage, stir and continue to bake, uncovered, for an additional ½ hour.

*Serves 4.*

# VERSATILE HAMBURGERS

*So named because you can make either hamburgers or meatballs with the same recipe.*

**½ pound lean ground beef**

**1 egg**

**2 tablespoons oatmeal**

**2 tablespoons wheat germ**

**¼ teaspoon salt**

**⅛ teaspoon black pepper**

**⅛ teaspoon garlic powder**

**2 hamburger buns**

Utensils needed

**small bowl**

**medium frying pan**

**spatula**

1. Place all ingredients (except buns) in a small bowl and mix well—get right in and squish well with your clean hands.
2. Form into two patties.
3. Place in frying pan with a spatula over medium heat and cook the patties for 4 to 5 minutes on each side.
4. Remove from the pan with a spatula and place on toasted or plain, buttered hamburger buns. Add your favorite topping and eat.

*Serves 2.*

Suggested Toppings: *Sliced raw onion, sliced raw tomatoes and lettuce, cheese slices, crisply cooked bacon slices, sliced pickles, mustard, and ketchup are all great accompaniments.*

Note: *One-fourth cup of bread crumbs may be substituted for the combination of wheat germ and oatmeal.*

## MEATBALLS

*Use the preceding basic recipe but, instead of forming patties, shape into 1¼-inch balls and place in a baking pan. Turn oven to 450 degrees F, and when oven has reached this temperature (indicator light goes out), place meatballs in oven for 15 minutes. When done, they should be slightly pink in the center. (To test: Remove one meatball and cut in half.) One-half pound ground beef–this is about 1 cup–makes roughly 12 to 14 meatballs. These freeze well and are useful to have on hand for quick recipes like the following.*

### Quick Spaghetti and Meatball Dinner

*Thaw meatballs (take them out of the freezer in the morning to cook them that evening); simmer for about 20 minutes in canned spaghetti sauce. Pour over cooked spaghetti.*

## MOM'S MEAT LOAF

*This is a complete meal—a very nice feature! However, if you prefer having a baked potato and a green vegetable with your meat loaf, see the variation below. The Sweet Tomato Glaze is delicious!*

**1¼ pounds lean ground beef**
**⅔ cup evaporated milk**
**½ cup fine fresh bread crumbs or cracker crumbs**
**½ cup finely chopped onion**
**¼ cup ketchup**
**1 teaspoon salt**
**¼ teaspoon pepper**
**2 teaspoons Worcestershire sauce**
**3 medium potatoes**
**3 medium carrots**
**2 teaspoons dried parsley flakes or chopped fresh parsley**

Utensils needed

**medium bowl**
**small roasting pan or large shallow baking dish**
**vegetable peeler**

1. Turn oven to 375 degrees F.
2. Combine the meat, milk, crumbs, onion, ketchup, salt, pepper, and Worcestershire sauce in a bowl; blend really well (hand blending works best).
3. Shape the mixture into a loaf and place in the center of a small roasting pan or a shallow baking dish.

4. Peel the potatoes and carrots, cut into ¼-inch slices, and arrange in layers around the meat.
5. Sprinkle with additional salt and pepper (roughly 1 teaspoon salt and ¼ teaspoon pepper).
6. Sprinkle top layer with chopped parsley.
7. Cover pan tightly with foil or lid.
8. Bake at 375 degrees for 1 hour or until vegetables are fork-tender.
9. Uncover and bake an additional 10 minutes to brown the meat.

*Serves 4.*

*Variation:* If you decide to delete the vegetables, the meat loaf can be baked in a 9- by 5-inch loaf pan. Bake at 350 degrees F, uncovered, for 45 minutes. Drain off any fat (place a plate over top so your loaf doesn't land in the sink). Cover top with Sweet Tomato Glaze (see below) and return to oven for an additional 15 to 20 minutes.

## Sweet Tomato Glaze

**¼ cup ketchup**

**1 teaspoon dry mustard**

**½ cup brown sugar**

## Utensils needed

**small bowl**

1. Put all of the glaze ingredients in a small bowl and stir to dissolve sugar.

# SPAGHETTI SAUCE

**1 medium onion**

**1 small green pepper**

**2 tablespoons olive oil**

**1½ pounds ground beef**

**¼ pound fresh mushrooms**

**1 teaspoon oregano**

**¼ teaspoon garlic powder**

**2 cans spaghetti sauce, any variety (14 ounces each)**

Utensils needed

**chopping knife**

**Dutch oven or large pot**

**can opener**

1. Chop onion and green pepper.
2. Pour olive oil into the bottom of the Dutch oven (or large pot) and set over medium heat.
3. Add onion and green pepper and fry gently until soft.
4. Add ground beef. Cook until all trace of pink disappears, stirring occasionally.
5. Add mushrooms and sprinkle with oregano and garlic powder.
6. Turn heat to low before adding the canned spaghetti sauce.
7. Simmer, covered, for 30 minutes, stirring occasionally.
8. Serve over hot cooked spaghetti. (Follow directions for cooking on the spaghetti package.)

*Serves 4 to 6.*

*Suggested Accompaniments:* Caesar Salad, Cheesy Garlic Bread.

## ONE-STEP LASAGNE

*Actually, it's three steps. Don't be afraid to tackle lasagne just because you are a beginner. This recipe was designed for you and eliminates cooking the noodles beforehand, which most people find the most tedious job of all. (The noodles have a tendency to tear unless you cook them perfectly; they also love to slip into the sink when you are trying to drain them.)*

**2½ cups grated mozzarella cheese**

**2 cups dry-curd cottage cheese**

**1 egg**

**1 teaspoon salt**

**½ teaspoon oregano**

**1 jar (28 ounces) spaghetti sauce**

**½ package (1 pound) uncooked lasagne noodles**

**⅔ cup water**

Utensils needed

**grater**

**medium bowl**

**9- by 13-inch baking dish**

**scissors**

1. Set aside ½ cup of the mozzarella cheese for the top of the casserole.
2. Combine the cottage cheese, remaining 2 cups mozzarella cheese, egg, and salt in a bowl.
3. Add oregano to spaghetti sauce. Spread ⅔ cup of this sauce over the bottom of the baking dish. It won't cover every inch, but don't worry and don't be tempted to add more.
4. Place five of the dry noodles (this is half the required quantity) over this in a single layer—four lengthways and

one crossways. (The crossways one will be a little too long so cut a bit off the end with sharp scissors.) The noodles won't cover every inch of the pan, but they do swell a bit, and you want a little space around the edges of the pan because this is where you are going to pour the water just before the dish goes into the oven.

5. Place half of the cheese mixture on top of the noodles.
6. Pour another ⅔ cup of sauce over the cheese mixture.
7. Lay remaining noodles on top of spaghetti sauce and top with remaining cheese mixture.
8. Pour remaining sauce over all. Last, top with the ½ cup of saved grated cheese.
9. The uncooked dish can sit all day in the refrigerator or overnight if you wish.
10. Just before baking, heat the oven to 350 degrees F.
11. Pour the water around the edge of the casserole, cover, and bake for 1 hour.
12. After removing the lasagne from the oven, let it sit for 20 minutes before cutting it into serving pieces. This is important!

*Serves 6.*

Note: *This recipe doubles very well and freezes well after cooking.*

*Suggested Accompaniments:* Tossed Green Salad and Cheesy Garlic Bread.

*Variations:*

1. Add 1 pound ground beef to the spaghetti sauce. Cook the ground beef first by gently frying until the red has disappeared. Drain off fat.
2. Combine 1 package frozen spinach with the cheese mixture.

## CHILI

*Our friend Sheilah is gorgeous and has the tidiest kitchen you'll ever see—and why not?—she never cooks. Although she has been married for 25 years, our Sheilah can still be classified as an "absolute beginner." She does, however, make one thing—the best chili—and if she can, we know you can! It makes a large amount, but it's great party fare. You can freeze any unused portions in small containers.*

**2 pounds lean ground beef**
**4 medium-size onions**
**2 medium-size green peppers**
**3 cans (14 ounces each) kidney beans, drained**
**2 packages (envelopes) chili mix**
**3 cans (10 ounces each) button mushrooms, drained**
**2 cans (10 ounces each) tomato soup**
**2 cans (14 ounces each) tomatoes**
**¼ cup white vinegar**
**1 teaspoon chili powder**
**3 dried red chili peppers**
**1 teaspoon salt**
**½ teaspoon pepper**

Utensils needed

**Dutch oven**
**sharp knife**
**can opener**

1. Sauté ground beef in Dutch oven or large pot until meat loses its pink color. Drain off any fat that accumulates in the bottom of the pan.

2. Cut onions into large chunks—about eight per onion. Add to ground beef and sauté until onions turn transparent in color.
3. Cut green peppers in half, remove seeds, and discard. Cut each half into large chunks and add to pot. Continue sautéing for 2 to 3 minutes.
4. Add drained kidney beans, chili mix, and drained mushrooms.
5. Stir in tomato soup, canned tomatoes, vinegar, and chili powder.
6. Crush dried chili peppers between your fingers and add. (Do *not* touch your eyes until you have washed your fingers!)
7. Stir in salt and pepper and continue to simmer for about 30 minutes, stirring occasionally.

*Serves 12.*

Note: *We like the "chunky" vegetables, but they are not really typical of chili. If you think you would like a finer texture, by all means chop the vegetables into smaller pieces.*

# MARY'S 1-2-3 CASSEROLE

*You can prepare steps 1 and 2 before you go to work in the morning, then put the finishing touches on just 35 minutes before you plan to serve it. This dish is good enough to serve to guests and tastes much better than you'd expect.*

Step 1

- **1 to 1¼ pounds lean ground beef**
- **1 cup sliced fresh mushrooms**
- **½ cup chopped onion**

Step 2

- **½ teaspoon salt**
- **½ teaspoon pepper**
- **1 small can (7½ ounces) tomato sauce**
- **1 cup grated sharp Cheddar cheese**

Step 3

- **¼ teaspoon oregano**
- **¼ teaspoon basil**
- **½ cup light sour cream**
- **1 can Pillsbury Crescent Rolls**

Utensils needed

**medium frying pan**

**grater**

**8- or 9-inch square baking dish**

**Step 1:**

1. In a medium frying pan, cook the ground beef, mushrooms, and onion together until all trace of pink disappears from the beef.

**Step 2:**

2. Remove from heat and stir in the salt, pepper, and tomato sauce, empty into a square baking dish (8- or 9-inch), and cover top with grated cheese.
3. Cover with plastic wrap and put in fridge until chilled–all day is fine.

**Step 3:**

4. When ready to assemble, turn oven to 350 degrees F.
5. In a small dish or measuring cup, stir the oregano and basil into the sour cream (you can do this ahead as well).
6. Separate eight crescent rolls into triangles and distribute sour cream equally, spreading with back of spoon over each triangle. Roll up each one, starting at wide end (crescent shape), and arrange over top of casserole.
7. Bake, uncovered, at 350 degrees for 30 minutes or until rolls are golden brown.

*Serves 4.*

## PAN-FRIED PORK CHOPS

*Chops from the loin are the choicest.*

**2 pork chops, 1 inch thick**

**2 tablespoons water**

Utensils needed

**sharp knife**

**small frying pan with lid (most frying pans do not come with a lid, so find one from a saucepan that will fit)**

1. Trim excess fat from chops.
2. Heat a small frying pan over medium heat and rub the inside with a piece of the fat you have trimmed from the chops until the pan looks well greased.
3. Brown chops fairly slowly on both sides, roughly 3 minutes each side.
4. Add water to frying pan and *cover* tightly.
5. Turn heat to low and continue cooking for 30 minutes.

*Serves 1 or 2.*

Note: *Thin chops require no water; cover tightly and reduce cooking time to 20 minutes if your chops are thinner than 1 inch.*

*Suggested Accompaniments:* Baked Potato, Carrots and Brussels Sprouts, applesauce.

# PORK CHOP & RICE BAKE

**4 to 6 pork chops**

**1 can (10 ounces) cream of chicken soup**

**½ soup can of milk**

**1 cup instant rice, uncooked**

Utensils needed

**large frying pan**

**9-inch square baking dish**

**can opener**

1. Turn oven to 350 degrees F.
2. Brown chops in the frying pan over medium heat.
3. Remove chops from frying pan and arrange in a baking dish.
4. Combine soup, milk, and rice and pour over chops.
5. Cover with a lid, if your baking dish has one, or aluminum foil folded tightly over the edges to fit snugly.
6. Place in oven and bake, covered, for 1 hour.

*Serves 4.*

*Suggested Accompaniment:* Carrots and canned peas (petit pois—the very best canned peas available; some people prefer them to fresh or fresh frozen; just heat and serve).

## INSTANT BARBECUED SPARERIBS

*Simply prepared, simply scrumptious. This is one of those good news, bad news stories. The good news is that when we tried these, our families raved, "Gee, Mom, these are the best barbecued spareribs you've ever made!" The bad news was that we had spent 50 years, collectively, laboring over complicated 10- or 12-ingredient recipes for them before we found this incredibly easy one.*

**2 to 3 pounds lean back spareribs**

**1 onion**

**1 cup bottled barbecue sauce (your favorite brand)**

Utensils needed

**sharp knife**

**broiler pan or baking pan and rack**

**paper towels**

1. Cut ribs into sections of one or two ribs each.
2. Heat oven to 400 degrees F.
3. Place ribs on top rack of broiler pan. (Most ovens come with one.)
4. Cook ribs for 30 minutes, then turn ribs over and bake for another 30 minutes.
5. Reduce oven heat to 300 degrees F.
6. Remove broiler or baking pan from oven, and set the rack with ribs on it on paper towels. Pour out the accumulated grease from the broiler pan.

7. Cut the onion into large slices (if you like onions) or, if you don't want them to be so evident, dice onion small.
8. Add onions and barbecue sauce to broiler pan, then add ribs. Turn ribs over a couple of times to coat with sauce.
9. Bake for 1½ hours.

*Serves 4 to 6.*

*Suggested Accompaniments:* Hot fluffy rice, Glazed Carrots, green peas.

## JO'S MARINATED PORK TENDERLOIN

*This is a favorite weekend fare for daughter Mary Jo (champion swimmer), who would rather be doing just about anything else than cooking. She handles this delicious dish very well.*

**2 tablespoons sherry***

**1 tablespoon sugar**

**2 tablespoons soy sauce**

**1 tablespoon minced fresh ginger root**

**1 to 2 cloves garlic, minced**

**2 to 3 pork tenderloins (they weigh roughly ¾ pounds each, so you want about 2¼ pounds total weight)**

Utensils needed

**small bowl**

**baggie or covered casserole dish**

**barbecue or broiler pan**

1. Combine the marinade ingredients (sherry, sugar, soy sauce, ginger, and garlic) in a small bowl.
2. Pour marinade over meat and transfer the meat to a baggie or covered casserole dish. Let the meat marinate in the refrigerator for 4 to 6 hours.
3. Barbecue in a barbecue pan for 7 minutes on each side or until cooked (no less than 5 minutes and no more than 12 minutes depending on the size and temperature of the meat). If you prefer to broil under a preheated broiler, this method will take about the same time as barbecuing. If you are not comfortable with either method, the meat can be baked in an oven preheated to 325 degrees F for about 50 minutes.

* You may use cooking sherry in this recipe.

*Serves 4 to 6.*

Note: *You can store fresh ginger root in the freezer, grate it frozen (skin and all is even okay), and return the unused portion to the freezer.*

*Suggested Accompaniments:* Baked Potato or rice, fresh green beans, and a Tossed Green Salad (see page 91) with lots of cherry tomatoes for color.

# SAUSAGE & RICE CASSEROLE

*A favorite because of its versatility. May be cooked on the stovetop or in the oven. An excellent dish to accompany barbecued beef. The best feature, though: It doubles, triples, and quadruples for a crowd.*

**1 pound sausage meat**

**1 large onion**

**1½ cups long-grain rice, uncooked**

**2 cans (10 ounces each) button mushrooms, undrained**

**2 cans (10 ounces each) consommé**

**Fresh parsley (optional)**

Utensils needed

**sharp knife**

**large saucepan**

**can opener**

**large casserole**

1. Thaw the sausage meat, if frozen.
2. Chop the onion.
3. Cook sausage over medium heat in a saucepan until well browned.
4. Lower heat, add onion, and continue cooking until onion becomes transparent.
5. Add rice and cook until rice becomes golden-colored, stirring continuously.

6. Add undrained mushrooms and consommé.
7. Continue cooking at a low heat, stirring occasionally, until liquid has been absorbed, about 30 minutes, and until rice is cooked.
8. Transfer to a casserole to serve. Decorate with fresh parsley.

*Serves 6 to 8 as a main dish, 10 to 12 as a buffet accompaniment. Any leftover portion freezes well.*

*Variation:* If you prefer, after you have added the soup and mushrooms, transfer to a casserole, cover, and finish cooking in the oven about 35 to 40 minutes at 350 degrees F.

## APPLE-GLAZED PORK ROAST

**1 boneless pork loin roast (2 pounds)**

**¼ cup apple jelly, melted***

**2 tablespoons Dijon mustard**

**½ teaspoon garlic powder**

Utensils needed

**small rack**

**small shallow roasting pan**

**small brush (not necessary but helpful)**

1. Turn oven to 325 degrees F.
2. Trim excess fat from top of pork loin and place pork on a small rack** in a small shallow roasting pan.***
3. Combine melted jelly, mustard, and garlic powder and brush over roast. (Don't put all the glaze on at this stage; save enough to baste three more times.)
4. Bake, uncovered, for 1 hour and 55 minutes, basting every 30 minutes.
5. Let stand for 10 minutes before slicing.

*Serves 4 to 6.*

*Suggested Accompaniments:* Baked sweet potatoes, Broccoli, and corn.

* The easiest way to melt the jelly is in a glass measuring cup placed in the microwave on reheat for 1 or 2 minutes.

** A small round cake rack will fit in the roasting pan.

*** Lining the baking pan with foil makes clean-up easier.

# CABBAGE ROLL CASSEROLE

*Daughter Sheri's comfort food.*

**1½ pounds ground beef**

**2 medium onions, chopped**

**1 clove garlic, minced**

**1 teaspoon salt**

**¼ teaspoon pepper**

**1 can (14 ounces) tomato sauce (save can to measure water)**

**1 can (14 ounces) water**

**½ cup long-grain rice, uncooked**

**Butter or nonstick cooking spray**

**4 cups shredded cabbage**

Utensils needed

**medium to large covered saucepan**

**large covered baking dish or pan**

1. In a medium to large covered saucepan, brown the beef, onions, and garlic until no trace of pink remains in the beef.
2. Sprinkle with the salt and pepper.
3. Stir in the tomato sauce and water.
4. Bring mixture to a boil.
5. Stir in the rice.
6. Cover and simmer for 20 minutes.

7. Preheat oven to 350 degrees F.
8. Spray a large covered baking dish or pan with nonstick cooking spray (or grease with oil or butter).
9. Place ½ of the cabbage in the baking dish or pan and cover with ½ of the rice mixture.
10. Top rice mixture with remaining cabbage and then the remaining rice mixture.
11. Cover and bake for 1 hour.

*Serves 4 hungry people.*

*Suggested Accompaniment:* Sour cream on the side.

## BUSY DAY HAM WELLINGTON (WITH CANNED HAM)

*Great to serve as company fare or homestyle. Because the ham is enclosed in a biscuit dough, the flavors really penetrate. Also excellent served cold the following day.*

**1 canned ham**

**¼ cup liquid honey**

**¼ teaspoon ground cloves**

**¼ teaspoon dry mustard powder**

**1 package Pillsbury Crescent Rolls**

Utensils needed

**can opener**

**paper towels**

**small bowl**

**baking sheet**

1. Heat oven to 375 degrees F.
2. Open the can of ham and drain liquid from it.
3. Dry ham thoroughly by patting with paper towels.
4. Mix honey, cloves, and mustard powder together in a small bowl.
5. Open the crescent rolls according to package instructions.
6. Do not separate the dough triangles but lay the sheet of dough out on a counter and push together along perforation marks to make a solid rectangle of dough.
7. Set ham on dough and spread entire surface with honey mixture.

8. Fold sides of dough up over ham, pressing edges together, then turn the package over (so seam is facing down) to place on a baking sheet. Tuck dough under at both ends.
9. Bake at 375 degrees for 30 minutes. Crust will be golden brown.
10. To serve, transfer to a platter (use two spatulas) and cut into 1-inch slices.

*Serves 6.*

*Suggested Accompaniments:* Baked Acorn Squash (see page 273), Green Beans (see page 242), coleslaw.

## BROILED HONEYED HAM STEAK

**¼ cup orange marmalade**

**2 tablespoons liquid honey**

**1 center-cut ham steak, about 1-inch thick**

**8 whole cloves**

Utensils needed

**small bowl**

**small broiler pan***

1. Turn broiler on.
2. In a small bowl, stir together the marmalade and honey until well mixed. Set aside.
3. Score the outside fat of the ham by cutting through the fat at about 1-inch intervals, *almost* to the meat. This prevents it from curling. Stud the fat with cloves.
4. Place the ham steak on the broiler pan. With oven door open, broil about 3 to 4 inches from heat for 3 minutes on the first side. Turn ham over and spread uncooked side with the marmalade–honey mixture.
5. Broil the second side for 5 to 6 minutes or until it looks dark golden brown around the edges.

*Serves 2 to 3.*

*Suggested Accompaniments:* Baked Potato, creamed corn, Green Beans.

* If you have no small broiler pan, place a small wire trivet or cake cooler rack on a cookie sheet. If you spread foil on the pan first, it makes cleaning up a little easier.

# BROILED LAMB CHOPS

*Remember: When broiling, oven door is always left open. (Line the broiler pan with foil for easy cleaning.)*

**4 *loin* lamb chops, 1-inch thick**

**Garlic salt**

**Pepper**

Utensils needed

**broiler pan**

1. Turn broiler on.
2. Place chops on the broiler pan and, when broiler has been on for at least 5 minutes, place broiler pan on top rack in open oven and broil chops until brown, about 5 minutes. *Then* sprinkle the cooked side with garlic salt and pepper.
3. Turn and broil the uncooked side for an additional 5 to 6 minutes. Sprinkle with garlic salt and pepper.

*Serves 2.*

Note: *You want the chops slightly pink around the bone. Thicker chops will require a longer cooking time–1 or 2 minutes more each side.*

*Variation:* For *shoulder* lamb chops, cook exactly as for loin chops but marinate first in the following marinade.

**1 large clove garlic**

**½ cup oil**

**1 tablespoon white wine**

**⅛ teaspoon crushed rosemary**

1. Mince the garlic.
2. Combine all ingredients and pour over shoulder lamb chops in a shallow bowl. Let chops sit for 2 hours or more, turning once or twice during this time.
3. Remove from marinade and follow cooking instructions for loin chops.

*Serves 2.*

*Suggested Accompaniments:* Potatoes (baked or French fried), green peas, Cauliflower with Cheese Sauce or Broiled Tomato Halves, mint jelly.

## BAKED LAMB CHOPS

*If you have not yet christened your broiler and don't feel like experimenting with expensive lamb chops, you can bake them.*

**2 loin lamb chops***

**Worcestershire sauce (roughly 1 teaspoon per chop)**

**Fresh lemon juice (roughly 1 teaspoon per chop)**

**1 teaspoon butter per chop**

Utensils needed

**2-tined fork**

**small, shallow baking pan**

1. Poke holes all over lamb chops, then sprinkle with both the Worcestershire sauce and lemon juice. Top with butter.
2. Bake in the shallow baking pan in an oven preheated to 375 degrees F for 15 to 20 minutes. The meat will be pink, which is exactly how most lamb-lovers prefer it, for maximum texture and flavor. If you prefer your lamb well-done, increase the cooking time to 30 to 35 minutes.

*Serves 1 or 2.*

*Suggested Accompaniments:* Baked sweet potatoes and green peas.

* You might need two chops per person, depending on the size.

## BARBECUED BUTTERFLIED LEG OF LAMB

**1 leg of lamb (4 to 5 pounds), boned and butterflied***

Lamb Marinade

**1 clove of garlic, minced**

**2 tablespoons Dijon mustard**

**1½ teaspoons rosemary**

**¼ cup soy sauce**

**2 tablespoons olive oil**

Utensils needed

**9- by 13-inch baking dish**

**small bowl**

**barbecue**

**sharp knife**

1. Place lamb in a 9- by 13-inch baking dish.
2. Whisk all marinade ingredients together in a small bowl. Smear over both sides of lamb (more heavily on the cut side). Let sit for at least 1 hour.
3. Barbecue over medium coals for roughly 30 to 40 minutes (15 to 20 minutes each side, starting with the fleshy side) or until meat thermometer registers 150 to 160 degrees F. Cooking times will vary according to your grill, the temperature of the meat (whether at room temperature or right out of the fridge), the weather, preheat time, and so on. All things considered, the meat should be served pink and juicy.

* When you buy the lamb, tell the butcher you plan to barbecue, and he will be happy to do the butterflying, which means cutting the leg open and spreading it flat so all the meat is nearly the same thickness.

4. Let sit for 5 to 10 minutes, then slice on a slight diagonal and serve.

*Serves 6 to 8.*

*Suggested Accompaniments:* Oven-roasted potatoes, Broccoli with cheese sauce, and Greek Salad.

*Variation:* For Roast Leg of Lamb, leave leg whole. Mix 3 cloves garlic, minced, and 1 to 2 teaspoons lemon pepper into 2 tablespoons Dijon mustard and rub over roast. Transfer roast to a baking pan and bake at 325 degrees F for 3 hours. It is best to use a meat thermometer (150 to 160 degrees for medium).

## LIVER WITH ONIONS & BACON

*If you have been brought up to believe you should eat liver once a week, you must know how to cook it. Liver-lovers are fairly well split between those who insist it should be served with onions and those who feel it is best when served with bacon. This sauce will satisfy both.*

**1 pound calf's liver**

**4 slices bacon**

**3 tablespoons all-purpose flour**

**1 can (10 ounces) onion soup**

**4 tablespoons chili sauce**

***No salt***

Utensils needed

**electric frying pan or large frying pan with lid**

**paper towels**

**wax paper**

**can opener**

**small bowl**

1. Remove the thin outer skin from sliced liver. (Most liver purchased at the supermarket comes already sliced and most butchers slice it about ⅓-inch thick.)
2. Turn electric frying pan to 325 degrees F and fry bacon until crisp. If you are doing this in a nonelectric frying pan, place pan over medium heat to cook the bacon.
3. When bacon is cooked, remove to paper towels and pour off half the bacon fat from the pan.

4. Sprinkle flour on a piece of wax paper or plastic wrap; dip liver slices one by one in the flour, turning to coat both sides.
5. Cook liver in bacon fat in the frying pan over medium heat, about 2 to 3 minutes on each side, just enough to brown lightly. Liver toughens when it is overcooked, so don't overdo it.
6. Combine undiluted soup with the chili sauce in a small bowl. Tear bacon into 1-inch pieces and add to sauce.
7. Pour sauce over liver. Cover the frying pan, turn heat to low, and simmer the liver and sauce for 5 minutes.
8. Remove cover and simmer for an additional 5 minutes, just long enough to thicken sauce a bit.
9. Serve hot.

*Serves 4.*

*Suggested Accompaniments:* Mashed Potatoes, Green Beans, corn.

7

# Poultry Dishes

# ROAST CHICKEN

**4- to 5-pound roasting chicken**

**2 tablespoons oil**

**¼ teaspoon salt**

**¼ teaspoon pepper**

**¼ teaspoon thyme**

**¼ teaspoon sage**

Utensils needed

**paper towels**

**roasting pan or large baking dish with rack**

1. Heat oven to 375 degrees F.
2. Remove giblets from the chicken and reserve. (In the chickens you buy in the supermarket, the giblets have been placed in a small paper bag stuffed inside the chicken.)

## Helpful Hints

1. If you have no string for tying chicken or turkey before roasting, use dental floss. It is very strong and doesn't burn.
2. For tasty fried chicken, add 1 tablespoon chicken bouillon granules (soup base mix) to 1 cup flour and 1 teaspoon paprika. Dip or shake chicken pieces in this mixture and fry as usual. There is no need to add salt; the soup base is salty enough.
3. When you are browning chicken, don't overcrowd the pieces, as they tend to sweat.
4. You must always wash chicken under cold running water before using, and remember to trim all excess visible fat. A pair of sharp scissors works better than a knife. Dry on paper towels.

3. Run chicken under cold water and pat dry with paper towels inside and out.
4. At this point, either stuff dressing (recipe follows) into the body cavity or simply stuff with an onion cut in half.
5. Pour oil into a corner of the roaster, then, with your fingers, mix in the seasonings.
6. Transfer the chicken to the roaster and rub the oil-and-seasoning mixture all over the outside skin of the bird.
7. If you have stuffed the chicken, close the cavity by sewing together with a needle and thread (or you can use skewers). Draw the legs and wings close to the body and secure with string.
8. Place chicken, breast side up, on a rack in the roasting pan.
9. Bake uncovered in the oven at 375 degrees for 1½ to 2 hours if unstuffed. If stuffed, cook for 2 to 2½ hours.
10. Spoon the juice that accumulates in the pan over the chicken every 15 minutes during the last hour of cooking.
11. Chicken is done when, if you prick the meat near the thigh joint with a fork, the juices run clear yellow with no trace of pink. You also should be able to wiggle the leg bone freely. If you use a meat thermometer, insert it in the thickest part of the thigh, not touching a bone; chicken is done when it registers 185 degrees F.
12. Transfer bird to a platter. Remove string and thread or skewers. Let stand 10 minutes for easier carving.

*Serves 5 to 6.*

*Suggested Accompaniments:* Mashed Potatoes, Brussels Sprouts or peas, Baked Acorn Squash (see page 273).

# POULTRY STUFFING (OR DRESSING)

*Always allow about ¾ cup for each pound of poultry. The quantities here make enough stuffing for a 5-pound chicken.*

**1 large onion**

**½ cup butter or margarine**

**½ teaspoon salt**

**½ teaspoon sage**

**½ teaspoon thyme**

**¼ teaspoon pepper**

**2 tablespoons chopped parsley**

**¾ cup chopped celery**

**5 cups bread crumbs**

Utensils needed

**sharp knife**

**frying pan**

**J-cloth (or net stuffing bag–see page 176)**

1. Chop the onion coarsely.
2. Melt the butter in the frying pan, then add onion, salt, sage, thyme, pepper, parsley, and celery. Fry gently over medium heat, stirring constantly.
3. When onions have turned golden, remove pan from heat and add bread crumbs.
4. Blend well.
5. *To stuff the chicken:* Line the inside of the chicken cavity with a damp J-cloth that you have unfolded to a single thickness. Spoon dressing into the lined cavity. Pull the ends of the J-cloth together and tie, forming a bag.

6. When the chicken is cooked, it will be easy simply to pull the J-cloth bag out and empty dressing into a bowl to serve. (Don't try to use the J-cloth method on small frying chickens because the cavity is too small.)

*Makes 6 cups.*

Note: *Stuffing may be made up to a day in advance, but never stuff the bird prior to roasting time. It is also not advisable to store leftover dressing in poultry when it is cooked, so the J-cloth (bag) method serves two purposes.*

# GIBLET GRAVY

*For a supermarket chicken, the giblets are found in a paper bag, generally in the neck cavity of the chicken or turkey along with the heart and liver. Use only the giblets and heart. Feed the liver to the cat or your friend's cat.*

**Giblets from 1 chicken**

**Water**

**2 tablespoons all-purpose flour**

**Salt**

**Pepper**

Utensils needed

**small saucepan**

**large measuring cup**

**wooden spoon**

1. While chicken is roasting, place giblets and heart in a saucepan. Add enough cold water to cover and bring to a boil over high heat. Cover saucepan and reduce heat to low.
2. Simmer until giblets are tender when pierced with a fork, at least an hour.
3. Remove from heat, drain, and reserve broth for gravy.
4. Chop giblets finely. Discard the heart.
5. When the chicken is cooked, remove it to a serving platter. You will prepare the gravy in the roasting pan.
6. Add 1 cup of reserved giblet liquid to the pan drippings. Place the pan over medium heat and scrape browned particles free from the bottom. Pour mixture into a large measuring cup. The fat will rise to the top.

7. Spoon the fat off the mixture in the measuring cup, and measure 2 tablespoons of fat into the roasting pan. If you need more fat, use butter.
8. Add enough giblet juice to the drippings remaining in the measuring cup to make 1 cup.
9. Heat fat over medium heat. Stir in the flour with a wooden spoon and cook until bubbly.
10. Remove from heat and gradually stir in the giblet stock mixture from the measuring cup. Stir constantly until gravy boils and thickens.
11. Stir in the chopped giblets and season with salt and pepper to taste.

*Makes 1 cup.*

Note: *These quantities make 1 cup of gravy. If you wish to make more, use 2 tablespoons fat and 2 tablespoons all-purpose flour for each cup of liquid.*

# ROAST TURKEY

*Prepare the bird exactly as for Roast Chicken (page 169). Use the stuffing recipe on page 171, but note you will need ¾ cup stuffing for each pound of poultry. If you are cooking a large bird—more than 8 pounds—increase the ingredients proportionately.*

*The J-cloth method described on page 176 (to stuff a chicken) works well on smaller turkeys—up to about 10 pounds. For larger turkeys, see the note below.*

*There is nothing wrong with the packaged stuffing mixes. Simply follow package directions. You might add a can of drained sliced mushrooms or, if it is a large turkey, water chestnuts cut in large dice.*

*We prefer to cook turkeys at a lower temperature than chickens. The following timetable is a good guide for cooking stuffed turkey at an oven temperature of 325 degrees F:*

| *Pounds* | *Time* |
|---|---|
| 6–8 | 3¾–4 hours |
| 8–10 | 4–4½ |
| 10–12 | 4½–5 |
| 12–14 | 5–5½ |
| 14–16 | 5½–6 |
| 16–18 | 6–6½ |
| 18–20 | 6½–7½ |
| 20–24 | 7½–9 |

*If you plan to cook the turkey unstuffed, allow 5 minutes per pound less cooking time.*

Note: *A turkey stuffing bag is an invaluable item to have on hand when dressing a large bird. The stuffing is placed inside the bag, which is tied with string and placed in the turkey cavity. When the turkey is cooked, simply remove the bag and empty stuffing into a serving dish. It is not advisable to leave any stuffing inside poultry after it is cooked; this method removes the stuffing entirely.*

*To make a stuffing bag you will need about half a yard of 45-inch-wide netting. Cut into six rectangles of 9 by 15 inches. Fold each rectangle in half along the longest edge and sew up two sides. You now have several inexpensive bags for your use. They are washable and make a dandy gift!*

# VICTOR'S CHICKEN

*To quote Victor (a swinging young bachelor when he gave us this recipe): "I come home from work, stick a potato and this chicken into the oven, and 10 minutes before it is finished, I cook a package of frozen broccoli. I sit down to dinner and it is so good I can't believe I made it!"*

**1 cut-up chicken (2½ to 3 pounds)**

**½ cup ketchup**

**¼ cup brown sugar**

**¼ cup water**

**1 package dry onion soup mix**

Utensils needed

**sharp knife**

**shallow baking dish**

**small mixing bowl**

**aluminum foil**

1. Turn oven to 400 degrees F.
2. Wash and dry chicken well. Trim excess fat.
3. Place chicken in a single layer in a shallow baking dish.
4. Mix together the ketchup, brown sugar, water, and onion soup mix in small bowl; spoon mixture over chicken.
5. Bake chicken, covered with foil, for 45 minutes.
6. Remove the foil and bake an additional 15 minutes.

*Serves 4.*

# HERB-BAKED CHICKEN

*If you are really pressed for time, this recipe will be invaluable. Any leftover portion is nice cold the next day.*

**2½ to 3 pounds cut-up chicken**

**⅓ cup melted butter**

**Salt**

**Pepper**

**Sweet basil**

**Thyme**

Utensils needed

**shallow baking dish**

1. Turn oven to 400 degrees F.
2. Brush chicken with melted butter on both sides and place *skin side down* in a shallow baking dish in a single layer.
3. Sprinkle with salt, pepper, sweet basil, and thyme.
4. Bake uncovered at 400 degrees for 30 minutes.
5. Turn *skin side up,* sprinkle with additional salt, pepper, sweet basil, and thyme, and bake for an additional 30 minutes. The skin will crisp up nicely and have a delightful flavor.

*Serves 4.*

*Suggested Accompaniments:* Rice or Baked Potato, Green Beans or peas, Tossed Green Salad.

# CHICKEN WELLINGTON

**1 package (1 pound) frozen puff pastry, defrosted**

**1 package (4 ounces) cream cheese, room temperature**

**2 whole chicken breasts**

**2 tablespoons butter**

**Salt**

**Pepper**

**⅛ teaspoon garlic powder**

**2 tablespoons chopped parsley**

Utensils needed

**sharp knife**

**small frying pan**

**small bowl**

**rolling pin**

**cookie sheet**

1. Make sure the puff pastry is thawed and the cream cheese has been left out at room temperature for a while.
2. Turn oven to 425 degrees F.
3. Peel off the skin from the chicken breasts. Cut cleanly along the center of the breastbone with a very sharp knife and, sliding the knife across the bone the whole way, cut meat away from bone. (For a more detailed description of how to bone chicken breast, see page 188.) You will now have four pieces of boneless, skinless chicken.
4. Melt butter in a small skillet over medium heat and fry chicken breasts gently for 2 to 3 minutes on each side. Chicken should be cooked through by this time. Sprinkle lightly with salt and pepper as they are cooking.

5. Remove chicken from frying pan and let cool to room temperature while you prepare the remaining ingredients.
6. Combine cream cheese, garlic powder, and parsley in a small bowl. A mixer is handy for this but not necessary. Mix until smooth and creamy.
7. Roll out pastry according to directions on package and cut into 4 rectangles 8 by 6 inches each.
8. Divide cream cheese mixture in four and spread one portion of mixture lengthwise down the middle of each rectangle of pastry. Place chicken breasts on top of this.
9. Moisten edges of pastry with water, bring pastry up over chicken, and pinch edges together to seal. Place seam side down on the ungreased cookie sheet.
10. Bake for 25 minutes or until pastry is golden brown.

*Serves 3 to 4.*

*Suggested Accompaniments:* Glazed Carrots, package of frozen spinach soufflé (follow directions on package).

## BAKED CHICKEN PIECES

*For when you really have no time or inclination to fuss. It is tasty enough to serve at a party, too.*

**2½ to 3 pounds cut-up chicken**

**1 package (1.5 ounces) dehydrated onion soup mix**

**1½ tablespoons butter**

Utensils needed

**large shallow baking pan**

1. Turn oven to 350 degrees F.
2. Place chicken pieces in a single layer in a shallow baking pan.
3. Sprinkle chicken with dry onion soup mix and dot with butter.
4. Cover chicken with foil and bake in oven at 350 degrees for 1 hour.

*Serves 4.*

*Suggested Accompaniments:* Hot fluffy rice (spoon some of the sauce from the baking pan over the rice), Tossed Green Salad.

# CHICKEN STIR-FRY

*Simple to prepare, eye-appealing, and low-cal to boot.*

2 tablespoons fresh lemon juice

2 tablespoons vegetable oil

Pinch of ginger or ¼ teaspoon grated fresh ginger*

½ pound boneless chicken breast, cut in long strips

3 green onions, cut in 1½-inch lengths

1 small green pepper, cut in long strips (discard seeds)

1 small red pepper (sweet), cut in long strips (discard seeds)

¼ pound pea pods

8 fresh mushrooms, cut in quarters

3 tablespoons cold water

1 tablespoon cornstarch

½ teaspoon sugar

2 tablespoons white wine

¼ cup cashews (optional)

Utensils needed

medium bowl

small bowl (or cup)

large frying pan or wok

wooden spoon

grater

* The flavor of this dish is improved considerably by using the fresh ginger root rather than the powdered ginger. (If you don't know what it looks like, ask your produce manager.) Peel a small piece and grate it onto a piece of wax paper or plastic wrap. Measure out ¼ teaspoon and add it to the marinade.

1. Combine lemon juice, oil, and ginger in a medium-size bowl.
2. Add chicken strips; stir to coat and let sit for 30 minutes to 1 hour to marinate.
3. Clean vegetables and cut up as specified above.
4. Place the water in a cup or small bowl; stir in cornstarch, then sugar, then wine. Set aside until needed during the final stage of cooking.
5. Place a large frying pan or wok over high heat and add chicken plus marinade. Stir constantly with a wooden spoon until chicken changes color (it will turn whitish); this will take only 2 to 3 minutes.
6. As soon as chicken looks cooked, stir in the green and red peppers, green onions, and pea pods. Continue to cook over high heat, stirring most of the time, for an additional 3 minutes.
7. Stir in the mushrooms (these don't take as long). Cook for another minute or two.
8. With your wooden spoon, push vegetables and chicken to sides of pan and pour the cornstarch-water mixture into center of pan. Cook, stirring this liquid constantly until it boils and thickens. (If you use cashews, add now.)
9. Stir vegetables around in this mixture until coated. (Avoid overcooking the vegetables since tender-crisp and colorful vegetables are the sign of a good stir-fry!)

*Serves 2 to 4.*

*Suggested Accompaniments:* Boiled rice or *our* favorite: served over cooked fettuccine noodles.

## CRUNCHY DRUMSTICKS

**1 cup cornflake crumbs**

**¼ cup sesame seeds**

**½ teaspoon salt**

**¼ teaspoon pepper**

**2½ to 3 pounds chicken drumsticks**

**3 to 4 tablespoons mayonnaise (not lowfat)**

Utensils needed

**small dish**

**shallow baking dish**

1. Turn oven to 350 degrees F.
2. Combine cornflake crumbs, sesame seeds, salt, and pepper in a small dish.
3. Coat chicken lightly with mayonnaise. You can use the back of a spoon, a knife, or—better still—your clean fingers!
4. As you coat the drumsticks, roll them in the cornflake mixture, then place them side by side in a shallow baking dish.
5. Bake uncovered for 30 minutes, remove from oven, and turn carefully with a metal spatula. Return to oven for an additional 30 to 35 minutes.

*Serves* 4 *to* 5.

*Suggested Accompaniments:* Baked Potato, steamed carrots, and a green salad.

*Helpful Hint: You can put the cornflake mixture in a medium-size plastic bag and shake the chicken pieces to coat. If you haven't purchased ready-made crumbs, you can make your own quite easily by putting cornflakes in a plastic bag and crushing them with a rolling pin.*

## BUSY DAY CHICKEN

*This dish was designed for those days when your horoscope advises to take it easy. It is a complete meal and is prepared quickly and easily.*

**2 medium onions**

**2 medium potatoes**

**3 medium carrots**

**1 tablespoon butter**

**2 tablespoons oil**

**2½ to 3 pounds cut-up chicken**

**2 teaspoons garlic powder**

**2 teaspoons oregano**

**1 cup water**

**Salt**

**Pepper**

Utensils needed

**sharp knife**

**vegetable peeler**

**electric frying pan or Dutch oven**

**spatula**

1. Chop the onions, and pare and quarter the potatoes and carrots.
2. Place butter and oil in a frying pan or Dutch oven, then turn heat to medium.
3. Add onion and cook until onions are soft—about 5 minutes.
4. Push onions aside a bit with a spatula and add chicken pieces.

5. Sprinkle with 1 teaspoon of garlic powder and 1 teaspoon oregano and brown slightly, for about 5 minutes.
6. Turn chicken over and sprinkle with remaining garlic powder and oregano. Brown this side slightly for an additional 4 minutes.
7. Add potatoes, carrots, and water. Sprinkle with salt and pepper. Place lid on and turn heat to high, just long enough until water starts to boil (you will hear it and see the steam).
8. Turn heat to low and simmer for 35 minutes.

*Serves 3 to 4.*

## SWISS-BAKED CHICKEN BREASTS

*If you like chicken, cheese, and mushrooms, and if you like simple dishes, we recommend the following.*

**Salt**

**Pepper**

**2 whole chicken breasts**

**8 fresh mushrooms**

**2 tablespoons chopped fresh parsley**

**4 slices Swiss cheese**

**4 slices mozzarella cheese**

Utensils needed

**9-inch square, shallow baking dish**

1. Turn oven to 350 degrees F.
2. Bone and skin the breasts (see next recipe, or you can buy breasts already boned). You should now have four pieces of skinless, boneless chicken.
3. Sprinkle the chicken pieces lightly with salt and pepper and place in a shallow baking dish in a single layer.
4. Wipe the mushrooms. Slice them over the chicken, then sprinkle with parsley.
5. Top each piece of chicken with a slice of Swiss cheese, then a slice of mozzarella cheese.
6. Bake for 40 to 45 minutes.

*Serves 3 to 4.*

*Suggested Accompaniments:* Hot fluffy rice, French-style green beans, Tossed Green Salad.

# GARNET'S BREASTS

*Simple yet elegant. If you are counting calories, omit the cream and it will still be excellent.*

- **2 whole chicken breasts**
- **½ cup bread crumbs***
- **¼ cup wheat germ**
- **¼ teaspoon thyme**
- **2 tablespoons oil**
- **2 tablespoons butter**
- **½ cup sherry**
- **¼ cup whipping cream**

Utensils needed

- **sharp knife**
- **shallow bowl**
- **large frying pan**
- **9-inch square, shallow baking dish**

1. Bone and skin the breasts.** (You can buy breasts already boned, but with a pair of kitchen shears and a sharp knife, it is a simple procedure and not so costly.)

* Use day-old bread for the crumbs instead of buying the dry packaged bread crumbs.

** To bone a chicken breast, place the whole breast skin side down. Locate the wishbone, which will be in the center of the thickest part of the breast, right at the front. With sharp shears, cut breast lengthwise in half, through the bone. Insert a sharp knife under the first rib in the rib cage and, with a scraping motion, separate the meat from the bone, working toward the thickest part.

2. Mix bread crumbs, wheat germ, and thyme in a shallow bowl.
3. Firmly press each chicken piece into this mixture to coat both sides.
4. Refrigerate until ready to cook. Chicken should sit in the refrigerator for at least 15 minutes to set the crumbs so they will adhere better during frying.
5. When you are ready to cook the breasts, turn oven to 350 degrees F.
6. Heat oil and butter in the frying pan over medium heat. When butter starts to sizzle, add chicken pieces and lightly brown on both sides. This will take about 3 to 4 minutes on each side.
7. Transfer to a baking dish in a single layer.
8. Add sherry to the frying pan and boil briskly until reduced by half, scraping up brown bits stuck to bottom. Reduce heat, add cream, and simmer for 2 minutes, stirring constantly. (Do not use half-and-half; it will curdle.)
9. Pour sherry sauce over breasts. Bake in preheated oven for 20 minutes. The breasts don't need to bake too long because they are mostly cooked from the frying.

*Serves 3 to 4.*

*Suggested Accompaniments:* Fine boiled noodles (follow instructions on package), Broiled or Baked Zucchini, fresh tomato slices sprinkled with your favorite salad dressing, and lots of chopped fresh parsley.

# JULIE'S CHICKEN

*This is commonly known at Julie's house as "Georgia Peach Chicken."*

Sauce

- 1 jar (8 ounces) peach jam
- ½ cup barbecue sauce
- ½ cup chopped onion
- 2 teaspoons soy sauce

Utensils needed

small bowl

1. Mix all the sauce ingredients together in a small mixing bowl and set aside while you prepare the chicken.

Chicken

- ½ cup flour
- ½ teaspoon paprika
- ½ teaspoon salt
- ½ teaspoon pepper
- 6 to 9 pieces of chicken
- 2 tablespoons oil
- 2 tablespoons butter
- 1 medium green pepper, seeded and sliced into thin strips

Utensils needed

plastic bag
large frying pan
large casserole dish

1. Turn oven to 350 degrees F.
2. Put flour in a plastic bag with the paprika, salt, and pepper.
3. Two to three pieces at a time, place each piece of chicken in the bag and shake to coat.
4. Heat oil and butter in a large frying pan and brown chicken on both sides.
5. Transfer chicken to a large casserole dish and cover with sauce.
6. Bake uncovered for 40 minutes.
7. Top with green pepper strips.
8. Reduce heat to 300 degrees and bake for an additional 5 to 10 minutes.

*Serves 4 to 5.*

## MARY JO'S "BEER BOTTOM CHICKEN"

*Cooking should be fun, and this currently very popular method for cooking chicken is proof of that. If you don't have a barbecue, this can be done successfully in the oven as well. The steam from the beer keeps the chicken moist, and the garlic and rosemary impart a subtle flavor to the meat. To capture that moisture and flavor, the neck portion of the chicken should be covered with foil or covered with a scooped-out onion or green pepper half.*

**1 small chicken, 3 to 3½ pounds**
**Oil or cooking spray**
**Seasoning salt (roughly 1 teaspoon)**
**½ can beer, room temperature**
**¼ cup oil**
**3 to 4 cloves garlic, minced**
**½ teaspoon rosemary**
**½ teaspoon salt**
**¼ teaspoon pepper**

Utensils needed

**aluminum foil**
**barbecue (unless you use the oven method below)**
**tongs**
**platter**

1. Remove and discard any fat inside the body and neck cavity of chicken.
2. Rinse chicken well with cold water and pat dry.
3. Spray outside of bird or rub with oil and sprinkle well with seasoning salt.

4. Uncap beer, pour out half, and place oil, garlic, rosemary, salt, and pepper into can with remaining beer.
5. Stand chicken upright and insert can into body. The chicken will be "sitting" on the beer can. Form a tripod by spreading out its legs then tucking each wing tip behind the chicken (the wing will fold back over itself at the first joint). Cover neck with foil.
6. Place directly on heated barbecue set at medium-low.
7. Cook for 1¼ to 1½ hours with lid down.
8. Use long tongs to remove chicken, as the beer can will be very hot. Place chicken on a platter and let it sit for 5 minutes, then carefully remove chicken from beer can and serve (the chicken, not the beer!).

### Oven Method

Prepare chicken as for barbecue but set it upright in a small shallow roasting pan or baking dish and bake in a preheated oven at 350 degrees F for 1½ hours.

*Serves 4.*

# TREV'S CHICKEN GUMBO

*Substitute 1 cup of diced leftover chicken for the freshly cooked chicken breast for a very tasty way to use up leftover chicken.*

**1½ to 2 tablespoons canola oil**

**½ cup diced onion**

**½ teaspoon garlic powder**

**6 ounces fresh skinless and boneless chicken breast, cooked***

**1 can stewed tomatoes (14 ounces)**

**½ medium-size green pepper**

**½ medium-size red pepper**

**½ teaspoon salt**

**¼ teaspoon pepper**

**½ cup water**

**1 cup minute rice, cooked (see instructions on box)**

Utensils needed

**medium-size saucepan**

**small saucepan**

1. Heat oil in a medium-size saucepan and sauté onion until tender. Sprinkle with garlic powder and stir.
2. Add all remaining ingredients except rice.
3. Cook rice according to directions on box.

* To cook the chicken breasts, heat about 1 to 2 teaspoons olive oil in a small skillet and sauté the chicken over medium heat for 2 to 3 minutes on either side or until no longer pink when cut near the center.

4. While rice is under way, bring chicken mixture to a boil and cook for 3 to 5 minutes. The chicken is already cooked, so just needs heating through, and you want the peppers to be tender-crisp. The fresh taste of this recipe is one of its nice features.
5. Put rice in individual bowls and spoon chicken mixture over top.

*Serves 2.*

# 8

# Seafood Dishes

Broiled Fish Steaks
Lowfat Halibut Steaks
Fried Fish Fillets
Fish Cakes
Baked and Barbecued Salmon (Fillets or Steaks)
Salmon Steaks
Boiled Shrimp
Broiled or Fried Shrimp
Curried Shrimp
Overnight Crab Casserole
Fillet of Sole
Baked Red Snapper or Cod Fillets
Linguine with Crab Sauce
Fettuccine Alfredo
Tuna Casserole
Linguine with Creamy Clam Sauce

## BROILED FISH STEAKS

*The most important thing to know about fish is the "nose test"–if you can smell it, it isn't fresh!*

**½ pound fish steak (salmon, halibut, or swordfish)**

**1 tablespoon melted butter**

**Salt**

**Pepper**

Utensils needed

**small baking dish**

### Helpful Hints

1. For cooking fresh fish by practically any method, use the timing rule of 10 to 12 minutes per inch of thickness, measured through the thickest part of the fish. To test for doneness, part the flakes of fish with a fork. If the flesh is milky and opaque all through the thickest part, it is cooked.
2. Fresh fish, other than shellfish, should be cooked at a high temperature for a short time whereas shellfish should be cooked gently. Avoid overcooking any kind of fish. Overcooked shellfish becomes tough, and other varieties of fish become dry and tasteless when overcooked.
3. To improve canned shrimp, soak them in ice water for one hour before using.
4. Add some chopped capers and a bit of lemon juice to mayonnaise for a tangy accompaniment to fish.

1. Turn broiler on about 10 minutes before cooking and arrange the oven rack so fish will be about 3 to 4 inches from the heat.
2. Brush steaks on *both* sides with the melted butter and salt and pepper. Place in a baking dish.
3. Broil (leaving oven door open) for 3 minutes on one side. Turn steak over and brush with additional butter on uncooked side; broil for an additional 3 minutes. *Do not overcook.* Fish steak is done when it flakes easily with a fork

*Serves 1.*

*Suggested Accompaniments:* Small boiled new potatoes or rice, spinach, broiled tomato halves (sprinkle with garlic salt and black pepper, dot with butter, and broil for 5 minutes), crusty French rolls.

## LOWFAT HALIBUT STEAKS

**2 tablespoons whole wheat flour**

**2 tablespoons sesame seeds**

**Nonstick olive oil cooking spray**

**2 halibut steaks**

Utensils needed

**small bowl**

**medium frying pan**

1. In a small bowl, combine the whole wheat flour and sesame seeds. Dip fish in this mixture to coat both sides.
2. Spray a medium frying pan well with nonstick olive oil cooking spray, then cook fish until done, about 4 minutes on each side over medium heat.

*Serves 2.*

# FRIED FISH FILLETS

**½ pound fish fillets (sole, haddock, bluefish, cod, perch)**

**1 egg**

**½ cup cracker crumbs**

**1 tablespoon oil**

**1 tablespoon butter**

**Salt**

**Pepper**

**Lemon wedges (optional)**

Utensils needed

**shallow bowl**

**wax paper or plastic wrap**

**medium frying pan**

**spatula**

1. Wash the fish and dry *thoroughly.*
2. Beat the egg in a shallow bowl.
3. Spread crumbs on a piece of wax paper or plastic wrap.
4. Dip fish in beaten egg, then "roll" in cracker crumbs.
5. Heat oil and butter in the frying pan (heavy pan is best) over moderate to high heat until butter starts to bubble but not burn.
6. Add fish and fry 3 minutes on the first side.

7. Sprinkle with salt and pepper, turn with a spatula, and fry for an additional 3 minutes on the other side or until fish is golden brown and flakes easily with a fork.
8. Serve at once with lemon wedges or tartar sauce.*

*Serves 2.*

*Suggested Accompaniments:* Hot fluffy rice, Tossed Green Salad.

*Variations:* This method may be used on scallops or oysters as well. Small whole fish such as smelt or trout should be rolled in cornmeal rather than cracker crumbs and cooked as above.

* For Easy Tartar Sauce, stir 2 tablespoons sweet pickle relish (the kind you put on hot dogs, but not the mustard type) into ½ cup mayonnaise. (Tartar sauce also is available ready-made at the supermarket.)

# FISH CAKES

*This makes a good supper dish and is a splendid way of using up leftover cooked fish. It is convenient if you just happen to have leftover mashed potatoes as well, but if not, the instant kind will do.*

**1 cup cooked fish**

**2 cups mashed potatoes***

**1 beaten egg**

**½ teaspoon salt**

**⅛ teaspoon pepper**

**2 tablespoons chopped fresh parsley (optional)**

**¼ cup all-purpose flour**

**2 tablespoons oil**

Utensils needed

**large bowl**

**paper plate or wax paper**

**frying pan**

**spatula**

1. Mash fish and potatoes together with the egg in a large bowl. Season with salt and pepper and add parsley.
2. With your hands, shape the fish mixture into cakes about 2½ inches in diameter and ½-inch thick.
3. Spread flour on a plate or piece of wax paper.
4. Dip both sides of cakes in the flour.

* Can use instant; follow directions on package.

5. Heat the oil in the frying pan and fry fish cakes on both sides, turning with a spatula, until golden brown, about 2 to 3 minutes on each side.

*Serves 2.*

*Suggested Accompaniments:* Peas, Tossed Green Salad.

*Variation:* Instead of cooked fish, you may use canned salmon (the cheapest brand, pink, is fine).

# BAKED AND BARBECUED SALMON (FILLETS OR STEAKS)

*The amounts of topping will vary depending on the size of the fish you are cooking, so use your judgment. Also use common sense when it comes to timing. For instance, a fish straight from the refrigerator will take a few minutes longer than fish that has been out on a counter in a warm kitchen for an hour. Remember: Fish is cooked when it is opaque through its thickest part.*

Fillet of Salmon

**Whole fillet of salmon***

**Butter or oil**

**Mayonnaise**

**Brown sugar**

**Soy sauce**

Utensils needed

**large, flat baking pan**

**pair of tweezers**

1. Turn oven to 375 degrees F.
2. Place fish fillet, skin side down, in a greased large, flat baking pan.
3. Smear the cut surface of the fish with mayonnaise in a thin layer.
4. Sprinkle brown sugar over the mayonnaise, also in a thin layer.

* Any butcher will fillet the salmon for you, but he may leave a few of the small bones. Rub your hand over the flesh of the fish (against the grain) and remove any stragglers with a pair of tweezers.

5. Sprinkle soy sauce over the brown sugar—enough to moisten the sugar well.
6. Place fish in the oven and bake for 8 minutes.
7. Turn broiler on, transfer fish to top rack in the oven, and finish cooking under the broiler for 3 minutes.

*Serves 1.*

Notes:

1. *It is a good rule of thumb to allow about ¼ pound of* boneless *fish per person.*
2. *This also is terrific on the barbecue if you have the hooded type. It will take 11 minutes. The fish will be wonderfully moist and flavorful. Most people tend to overcook fish, which is a big mistake.*

## Salmon Steaks

*You don't get the same "sealing off" of the flesh (skin on the bottom and mayonnaise and such on top), but it is still a nice way to cook this particular cut of fish. Steaks are usually cut 1-inch thick. They vary in width according to the size of the fish, but the following amounts are sufficient for steaks measuring 3 inches in width (not depth).*

**1 salmon steak**

**Butter or oil**

**1 tablespoon mayonnaise**

**2 teaspoons brown sugar**

**2 teaspoons soy sauce**

### Utensils needed

**large, flat baking pan**

*continues*

*continued from page 205*

1. Turn oven to 375 degrees F.
2. Place fish fillet, skin side down, in a greased large, flat baking pan.
3. Smear the cut surface of the fish with mayonnaise in a thin layer.
4. Sprinkle brown sugar over the mayonnaise, also in a thin layer.
5. Sprinkle soy sauce over the brown sugar—enough to moisten the sugar well.
6. Place fish in the oven and bake for 5 minutes.
7. Turn broiler on, transfer fish to top rack in the oven, and finish cooking under the broiler for 3 minutes.

*Serves 1.*

## Barbecued Salmon Steaks

**2 to 3 teaspoons fresh minced dill**

**1½ teaspoons grated lemon rind**

**¼ cup canola oil**

**4 salmon steaks (roughly 1-inch thick)**

**Salt**

**Pepper**

### Utensils needed

**grater**

**plastic bag**

**barbecue**

1. Stir fresh minced dill and grated lemon rind into canola oil, and marinate salmon steaks for anywhere from 2 to 8 hours (a plastic bag is great for this).
2. Remove from marinade, sprinkle with salt and pepper, and barbecue over medium heat for about 4 minutes on each side or until done. Salmon steaks are cooked when the flesh flakes and separates when prodded with a fork and is opaque throughout.

*Serves 4.*

# BOILED SHRIMP

*Most people, and not just beginners, tend to overcook shrimp. Don't overcook* any *fish. Remember, fish cooks very quickly, and shrimp are no exception. Cooking shrimp in their shells gives them a better shape; they curl up too much if you shell them first.*

**Water**

**Salt**

**Peppercorns**

**1 pound shrimp**

Utensils needed

**large saucepan**

1. Bring water to a boil in a large saucepan, making sure you have enough water to cover the shrimp well.
2. Add salt, using 1 tablespoon for every quart of water, and peppercorns (four should be enough).
3. Add shrimp to boiling water, turn heat down so water is just simmering, and then cover the pot. Cook for 3 minutes–no longer. Shrimp will be pink and tender at this point.
4. Drain immediately and chill.
5. Remove shells and the black vein (the intestine, harmless but unsightly).

*Serves 4.*

# BROILED OR FRIED SHRIMP

*The simplest preparations are usually the best when it comes to seafood.*

**1 pound shrimp**

**2 cloves garlic**

**2 tablespoons lemon juice**

**2 tablespoons finely chopped parsley**

**⅓ cup oil***

**Salt**

Utensils needed

**large bowl**

**large frying pan or shallow baking dish**

1. Peel and devein the shrimp (if you are using frozen shrimp, make sure they are thawed and well drained before cooking).
2. Mince the garlic, or chop very small, and combine with all the other ingredients, except shrimp, in a large bowl. Mix well.
3. Add shrimp and stir gently until shrimp are completely coated. You may cover with foil at this point and refrigerate until ready to serve. The actual cooking time will require no more than 6 minutes.

* Use olive oil if you have it, otherwise any vegetable oil.

**To Fry:** Arrange shrimp in a single layer in a frying pan and pour over them any oil mixture remaining in the bowl. Cook over high heat for 2 minutes, turning once. Sprinkle lightly with salt and cook for 1 additional minute.

**To Broil:** Turn broiler on at least 5 minutes before cooking the shrimp. When broiler is ready, place marinated shrimp in a single layer in a shallow baking dish and broil about 3 to 4 inches from heat for 2 to 3 minutes on each side. (Remember, always leave the oven door open when broiling.) Sprinkle lightly with salt.

*Serves 4.*

*Suggested Accompaniments:* Tossed Green Salad, sliced tomatoes, Uncle Ben's Long Grain and Wild Rice Mix, crusty French loaf.

## CURRIED SHRIMP

*If you feel like going native, add more curry powder.*

**1 pound shrimp, uncooked**

**½ medium onion**

**2 tablespoons butter**

**1 tablespoon all-purpose flour**

**¼ teaspoon salt**

**Pinch of white pepper**

**1½ teaspoons curry powder**

**⅛ teaspoon ginger**

**1 teaspoon sugar**

**2 tablespoons sherry**

**1 to 1½ cups milk**

Utensils needed

**chopping knife**

**large frying pan**

**wooden spoon**

1. Peel and devein the shrimp. (If you're using frozen shrimp, they will probably have been prepared. Make sure they are thawed before you cook them.)
2. Chop the onion.
3. Melt butter in the frying pan over medium heat.
4. Gently fry the onion and shrimp in butter until shrimp are cooked—they will turn pink. This will take no longer than 3 minutes.

5. Sprinkle shrimp with flour, salt, pepper, curry powder, ginger, and sugar. Stir with a wooden spoon until flour has been absorbed.
6. Add sherry and 1 cup milk and stir quickly and constantly until mixture bubbles and thickens. If you prefer a thinner sauce, add a little more milk and return to heat, stirring until mixture just reaches a slow boil. Remove from heat.

*Serves 3 or 4.*

*Suggested Accompaniment:* Serve with hot fluffy rice and an assortment of three or four condiments such as chopped banana, peanuts, raisins, chutney, fresh coconut chips, or chopped fresh peaches.

## OVERNIGHT CRAB CASSEROLE

*This is great for those busy days when you know you will be getting home late; you make your supper the night before! It is a good idea always to have a couple of hard-boiled eggs in the refrigerator. You will be surprised how often they come in handy. Put an X on the bottom of the hard-boiled ones to identify them easily.*

**1 can (6 ounces) crab**

**1 can (10 ounces) cream of chicken soup**

**⅓ cup milk**

**½ cup Miracle Whip**

**1½ teaspoons onion flakes***

**2 cups extra-fine noodles, uncooked**

**2 hard-boiled eggs**

**1 cup grated Cheddar cheese**

Utensils needed

**grater**

**can opener**

**medium mixing bowl**

**8-inch casserole**

1. Drain the crab, discarding juice. Empty crabmeat into a mixing bowl and break up slightly with a fork.
2. Stir in undiluted soup, milk, Miracle Whip, and onion flakes.
3. Stir in noodles; don't worry if some of them break.

* Comes in a small bottle to be found in the spice section of the supermarket.

4. Chop the eggs finely and stir into crab mixture, together with ½ cup of the cheese.
5. Empty into a buttered casserole dish. Top with remaining ½ cup cheese.
6. Refrigerate overnight.
7. At serving time, bake in an oven preheated to 350 degrees F for 30 minutes.

*Serves 4.*

*Suggested Accompaniments:* Tossed Green Salad, hot rolls.

## FILLET OF SOLE

**1 pound sole fillets***

**Oil**

**Salt**

**Pepper**

**1 tablespoon butter, melted**

**2 tablespoons chopped fresh parsley**

**2 teaspoons fresh lemon juice**

Utensils needed

**shallow baking dish**

**small dish**

1. Heat oven to 450 degrees F.
2. Place fillets in a lightly oiled, shallow baking dish, just large enough to hold the fish in a single layer.
3. Sprinkle lightly with salt and pepper.
4. In a small dish, combine butter, parsley, and lemon juice.
5. Spoon this mixture over the top of the fish.
6. Bake, uncovered, for 8 to 10 minutes. Serve at once.

*Serves 4.*

* If you are using fresh fish, make sure it is really fresh (use the nose test–there is no odor to fresh fish). If you use frozen fillets, first thaw, then dry them well with paper towels before placing them in the baking dish.

Note: *If you prefer to panfry the fish, keep it simple. Dip the fish fillets in flour (about 3 to 4 tablespoons), ¼ teaspoon salt, and ⅛ teaspoon pepper, mixed. Shake off the excess, then heat 1 tablespoon of butter and 1 generous tablespoon of vegetable oil together in a nonstick skillet. When the butter is well melted and starts to foam a bit, add fish and sauté for 3 minutes, turn the fish over carefully with a large spatula (the fish should be golden brown in color), then cook for an additional 3 minutes on the other side.*

*Suggested Accompaniments:* Hot fluffy rice, buttered spinach, cherry tomatoes, fresh lemon.

## BAKED RED SNAPPER OR COD FILLETS

**Nonstick vegetable oil**

**1 pound red snapper or cod fillets**

**⅓ cup plain yogurt**

**1 teaspoon prepared mustard**

**2 teaspoons finely chopped green onion**

**2 teaspoons dillweed (fresh if possible)**

**2½ tablespoons mayonnaise**

**¼ teaspoon salt**

**⅛ teaspoon pepper**

**2 tablespoons grated Parmesan cheese**

Utensils needed

**shallow glass baking dish**

**small bowl**

1. Heat oven to 450 degrees F.
2. Spray a shallow glass baking dish with nonstick vegetable oil.
3. Arrange fish in a single layer in the dish (thicker pieces to the outside), and fold any thin ends under a bit so the fish is fairly uniform in size.
4. In a small bowl, combine all of the remaining ingredients.
5. Spread this mixture evenly over the fish.
6. Bake, uncovered, for 12 minutes.*

*Serves 4.*

* Snapper and cod fillets are a little thicker than sole, so if you substitute sole in this recipe, test after 8 minutes. Fish is cooked when it flakes easily when tested with a fork.

Note: *If you use frozen fillets, dry them well with paper towels before placing them in the baking dish.*

*Suggested Accompaniments:* Broiled tomato halves, Green Beans, and Uncle Ben's Long Grain and Wild Rice Mix.

## LINGUINE WITH CRAB SAUCE

*Absolutely delicious and not a calorie, as you can see!*

**12 ounces linguine**

**½ cup butter**

**1 clove garlic**

**1 cup whipping cream**

**½ cup grated Parmesan cheese**

**1 can (6 ounces) crab, drained**

**½ teaspoon salt**

**¼ teaspoon black pepper***

**2 tablespoons chopped fresh parsley**

Utensils needed

**large saucepan**

**colander**

**serving platter**

**large frying pan**

**can opener**

1. Cook linguine according to package directions.
2. Drain well in a colander, then transfer to a serving platter.
3. While linguine is cooking, melt the butter in a large frying pan over low heat.
4. Mince the garlic and add to melted butter. Cook until garlic is soft.

* This is one case where freshly ground black pepper really does taste incomparably better than the packaged kind. So if you have a pepper grinder, use it!

5. Add cream and, stirring constantly, let it simmer until it starts to thicken a bit. This will take about 5 minutes.
6. Stir in the Parmesan cheese, drained crab, salt, and pepper. Stir over low heat until well heated through, about an additional 2 to 3 minutes.
7. Pour over cooked linguine and toss lightly.
8. Serve topped with chopped fresh parsley.

*Serves 4.*

## FETTUCCINE ALFREDO

*To transfer the previous dish into the classic "Fettuccine Alfredo," simply substitute fettuccine noodles for the linguine and delete the crab. Have a pepper grinder on hand for those who want a fresh grinding of pepper over the top.*

*Suggested Accompaniments:* Tossed Green Salad or Caesar Salad, crusty buns or good-quality French bread, fresh fruit plate for dessert.

*Variations:* You may substitute spaghetti for linguine. Cook according to directions on the package, but don't overcook. You want spaghetti cooked to the *al dente* (bitey) stage. How can you tell when the linguine or spaghetti is cooked? Remove one strand and throw it against the wall; if it sticks it is done. (This is no joke; a lot of people use this method!) If you don't fancy picking strands of cooked pasta off the wall, an alternative method is the thumb-and-forefinger test: The cooked strand should be slightly resilient, not mushy, when pressed between thumb and forefinger.

If you prefer to use fresh or frozen crab rather than canned, use 6 to 8 ounces.

# TUNA CASSEROLE

*A real family favorite, especially for the one cooking dinner.*

**1 package (10 ounces) frozen broccoli**

**Salt**

**1 can (7 ounces) tuna, flaked**

**1 can (10 ounces) cream of mushroom soup**

**½ soup can of milk**

**½ cup crushed potato chips**

Utensils needed

**medium saucepan**

**1½-quart baking dish**

1. Turn oven to 450 degrees F.
2. Cook broccoli in boiling, salted water in a medium saucepan until crisp-tender. Drain very well and place in a 1½-quart baking dish.
3. Drain tuna and arrange on top of broccoli.
4. Combine soup and milk and pour over tuna.
5. Sprinkle with potato chips.
6. Bake for 15 minutes.

*Serves 4.*

*Suggested Accompaniment:* Tossed Green Salad (see page 91).

## LINGUINE WITH CLAM SAUCE

*Don't leave out the fresh parsley—it's a must. To cook linguine, follow directions on the package. One pound will serve four to six people. Cook about ⅔ pound for the following sauce.* *See recipe on page 224 for Creamy Clam Sauce.*

**¼ cup quality olive oil**

**2 tablespoons butter**

**3 large cloves garlic, minced**

**¼ cup chopped fresh parsley leaves**

**¼ teaspoon crushed dried red chili peppers**

**2 cans (5 ounces each) baby clams, drained**

**¼ cup dry white wine**

**¼ cup grated Parmesan cheese**

**Hot cooked linguine (see introduction above)**

Utensils needed

**large frying pan**

**can opener**

**large pot for cooking pasta**

1. Put olive oil, butter, garlic, half the parsley (2 tablespoons), and chili peppers into a large frying pan. Cook for 2 minutes. (Watch the garlic! It mustn't burn or it will be bitter.)
2. Add the drained clams and wine and cook, uncovered, for 5 minutes.
3. Remove from heat and immediately stir in the Parmesan cheese and remaining parsley.
4. Toss with hot cooked linguine.

## Creamy Clam Sauce

**2 tablespoons butter**

**1 can (5 to 7 ounces) baby clams, drained**

**1 medium clove garlic, minced**

**1 can (10 ounces) cream of mushroom soup**

**½ cup milk**

**2 tablespoons chopped fresh parsley**

**8 ounces spaghetti or linguine, cooked (see directions on package)**

Utensils needed

**medium-size saucepan**

**can opener**

**large pot to cook pasta**

1. Melt butter in a medium-size saucepan.
2. Add the drained clams and garlic and cook gently for 5 minutes.
3. Stir in remaining ingredients and heat, stirring occasionally, until hot.
4. Toss with hot cooked spaghetti or linguine.

*Serves 2 to 3.*

# 9

# Vegetables

Asparagus
Roasted Asparagus
Broccoli
Stir-Fried Broccoli
Brussels Sprouts
Favorite Way with Cabbage
Carrots
Glazed Carrots
Cauliflower
Creamy Cauliflower
Corn-on-the-Cob
Green Beans (String Beans)
Green Bean Casserole
Sautéed Mushrooms
Barbecued Onions in Foil
Boiled Potatoes
Mashed Potatoes
Garlic Mashed Potatoes
Day-Before Mashed Potatoes
Party Mashed Potatoes (with Instant Potatoes)

Baked Potatoes
Roast Potatoes
Scalloped Potatoes
Quick Potatoes Romanoff
Oven-Baked Rice
Perfect Boiled Rice
Foolproof Method of Cooking Pasta
Chinese Snow Pea Pods
Broiled Tomatoes
Baked Tomato Halves
Mashed Turnip
Baked Zucchini
Roasted Root Vegetables
Sweet Potato Casserole (with Marshmallow Topping)
Baked Acorn Squash

## Helpful Hints

1. To remove skins from tomatoes, put them into boiling water for 1 minute to loosen skins, which will then peel off easily. Put peeled tomatoes into the refrigerator to firm them before slicing or chopping.
2. When cooking, vegetables grown below the ground should be started in cold water and vegetables grown above the ground started in boiling water.
3. To keep spaghetti and macaroni from boiling over, put a tablespoon of oil in the water.

# ASPARAGUS

*This is an elegant vegetable that at one time was available only in the spring. Cook extra because it is wonderful served cold the following day dressed with a little Vinaigrette Dressing (see page 106).*

**1 pound fresh asparagus**

**1 teaspoon salt**

**Melted butter (optional)**

Utensils needed

**large, sharp knife**

**vegetable peeler**

**skillet**

1. On a flat surface, line up asparagus spears side by side.
2. Using a large, sharp knife, evenly cut off tough, whitish bottoms and discard.*
3. Using a vegetable peeler, peel sides of thicker asparagus spears starting about 2 inches below the tips (young, thin asparagus does not need peeling). Set asparagus aside.
4. In a skillet, place enough water to cover asparagus when it is added. (To measure amount of water, place asparagus in skillet, barely cover with cold water, then remove the asparagus.)
5. Bring water to a boil, add 1 teaspoon salt, then add asparagus. Boil, uncovered, until tender-crisp–about 2 to 4 minutes after the water reaches second boil.
6. Drain and arrange on heated serving platter. Serve as is or with a little melted butter.

*Serves 4.*

* Some cooks like to break off the ends of the asparagus rather than cutting them off with a knife. The asparagus bends and breaks off easily at the most tender part of the stalk.

# ROASTED ASPARAGUS

*Roasting vegetables is very popular today, and asparagus is particularly delicious when you roast as follows.*

**1 pound asparagus spears (fat ones are best for roasting)**

**1 tablespoon extra-virgin olive oil**

**Salt**

**Freshly ground black pepper**

**2 tablespoons finely grated Parmesan cheese**

Utensils needed

**shallow baking pan**

1. Turn oven to 500 degrees F.
2. Break off tough ends of asparagus (where asparagus bends and easily breaks).
3. Wash well and peel bases if desired.
4. Place asparagus in a single layer in a shallow baking pan and drizzle with olive oil (roll around to coat spears on all sides).
5. Sprinkle lightly with salt and pepper.
6. Place asparagus in oven and roast for 8 to 10 minutes, until sizzling and starting to brown.
7. Remove pan from oven and sprinkle asparagus evenly with grated Parmesan (the cheese will melt on contact).
8. Serve immediately.

*Serves 4.*

## BROCCOLI

*We find the recipe for stir-frying broccoli (see page 231) to be the most popular way of preparing this vegetable, but if you are counting calories you might prefer it boiled or steamed. Broccoli should be soaked in salted water before cooking–1 teaspoon salt to 1 quart of water–to flush out the little forms of wildlife that sometimes hide in broccoli or cauliflower.*

**1½ pounds fresh broccoli**

**Water**

**Salt**

**Butter**

Utensils needed

**vegetable peeler**

**4-quart saucepan, or any large wide-mouth saucepan**

**rack (for steaming)**

To Boil Broccoli

1. Separate florets from the stem and set aside.
2. Using the vegetable peeler, pare the stalk; then slice into circles, about ¼- to ½-inch thick.
3. To a wide saucepan add about 1 inch of water (place your index finger in the pan and when the water comes up to your first knuckle, that is the right amount).
4. Add ¼ teaspoon salt to the water and bring water to a boil over high heat.
5. Add prepared broccoli–circles plus florets–to boiling water. Since you've just added cooler ingredients, the water will go off the boil momentarily.

6. When water returns to the boil, turn heat to medium, place a lid on the saucepan, and cook for about 10 minutes.
7. Test with a fork. When the fork enters the broccoli easily, it is cooked.
8. Drain immediately and serve topped with a spoonful of butter, which will melt on contact with the hot broccoli.

To Steam Broccoli

1. Follow the instructions above until you reach step 3. Now increase the amount of water to 2 inches. Bring to boil.
2. When water comes to a boil, place prepared broccoli in a steamer or on a rack above the boiling water. Cover and cook for about 15 minutes over high heat.
3. Test and serve as above.

*Serves 4.*

*Variation:* To dress up broccoli, serve topped with cheese sauce. This can be made very simply by heating 1 can (10 ounces) Campbell's Cheddar Cheese Soup, undiluted, with ½ cup grated sharp cheese until cheese has melted.

## STIR-FRIED BROCCOLI

*It is better to undercook broccoli than to overcook it, as with most vegetables.*

**1 pound fresh broccoli**

**1 clove garlic**

**3 tablespoons oil**

**Salt**

**Pepper**

**1 teaspoon sugar**

**½ cup water**

Utensils needed

**vegetable peeler**

**wok or frying pan with lid**

**spatula**

1. Separate florets from the stem and set aside. (You are going to add these later.)
2. Using the vegetable peeler, pare the stalk and then slice diagonally into circles, about ¼- to ½-inch thick. Mince or finely chop the garlic.
3. Heat oil, garlic, and a sprinkling of salt and pepper in the wok or frying pan. When hot, add broccoli circles. Fry over fairly high heat for about 2 minutes, stirring constantly with a spatula.
4. Sprinkle with sugar, add florets and water, and cover tightly. Cook for an additional 2 to 3 minutes or until cooked but still crisp.

*Serves 4 to 5.*

# BRUSSELS SPROUTS

*When buying brussels sprouts, look for green-colored, firmly closed ones. Avoid those with wilted leaves or with yellow or black spots.*

**1 pound brussels sprouts**

**2 teaspoons instant chicken soup mix**

**1½ tablespoons butter or margarine**

Utensils needed

**sharp knife**

**medium saucepan with lid**

1. Cut stems off brussels sprouts and pull off any wilted outer leaves.
2. Wash thoroughly.
3. Place 1 inch of water in the bottom of a saucepan (that's about a knuckle's depth).
4. Add chicken soup mix and bring to a boil. The chicken mix gives the sprouts a nice flavor, but if you do not have any on hand, substitute ½ teaspoon salt.
5. As soon as the water comes to a boil, drop in the brussels sprouts. Water will go off the boil for a moment.
6. When water returns to bubbling, place a lid on the saucepan and lower heat to medium. Continue cooking for 8 to 10 minutes or until just tender. *Do not overcook.* Test with a fork for doneness.
7. Drain the sprouts and immediately toss with butter.

*Serves 4.*

Note: *If you cut a shallow X into the stem end of the sprouts, they will cook more evenly and need a shorter time.*

# FAVORITE WAY WITH CABBAGE

*We will use a whole cabbage in this recipe because it is excellent reheated and, also, it is not possible to buy part of a cabbage! You may add cut-up, uncooked wieners to this recipe just before cooking and then it makes a great meal. Use as many wieners as you like–up to 1 pound.*

**1 medium onion**

**1 medium cabbage**

**2 tablespoons oil**

**1 tablespoon butter**

**2 tablespoons instant chicken soup mix**

**Salt**

**Pepper**

Utensils needed

**chopping knife**

**Dutch oven or electric frying pan**

1. Chop the onion finely.
2. Remove wilted outer leaves of cabbage and the hard core at the bottom and discard. Shred remaining cabbage.
3. Heat oil and butter in the Dutch oven or electric frying pan for 1 minute, then add the onion.
4. Turn heat to medium and cook onion for 1 minute.
5. Turn heat off before adding cabbage.
6. Sprinkle cabbage with the dry soup mix. Cover the pan.
7. Turn heat to high for 1 minute to start things steaming, then turn heat to low and cook for 10 minutes.
8. Remove cover and stir well.

9. Sprinkle lightly with salt and pepper—not too much salt because the chicken soup mix is salty. You may even omit the salt if you are sodium-conscious.
10. Replace cover and turn heat to high again for 1 minute, then back down to low for an additional 10 minutes.
11. Stir again and serve.

*Serves 4.*

Note: *If you use an electric frying pan, don't open the vent on the cover and don't be tempted to add water. You want the ingredients to "steam" together and retain all the goodness of flavor and nutrition. There should be enough moisture in the cabbage for this purpose. If you use a Dutch oven or a large pot that doesn't have a heavy bottom, do add ¼ cup of water, as thinner-bottomed pots have a tendency to burn things (a good thing to know if you haven't purchased all your pots yet).*

# CARROTS

*Next to the potato, the carrot is probably the most popular vegetable. Carrots really do help you to see in the dark, at least that is what both our mothers told us, and mothers are very wise.*

Utensils needed

**vegetable peeler**

**small saucepan**

Small Young Carrots (late spring/early summer)

**1 pound carrots**

**½ teaspoon salt**

**Butter**

Utensils needed

**sharp knife**

**medium saucepan**

1. Scrape with a knife or wash well.
2. Remove ends and place in salt and 1 inch of water in medium saucepan.
3. Turn heat to high until water is boiling, then turn heat to medium and continue cooking until carrots are tender when tested with a fork. This will take about 15 minutes, depending on the size of the carrots. You don't want them mushy.
4. Drain immediately. (Never let cooked vegetables sit in water.)
5. Toss with butter–1 teaspoon or more, to suit your taste.
6. Serve hot.

## Mature Carrots (winter)

1. Peel the carrots. (These usually have a tougher skin and require peeling with a vegetable peeler rather than the scraping method used on young carrots.)
2. Cut the peeled carrots into slices or dice, and follow procedure above. If they are thinly sliced, carrots should cook in 10 minutes.

*Serves 4.*

*Variations:*

1. Hot cooked carrots also may be mashed with a bit of butter and a pinch of either nutmeg or ginger.
2. If you are in a hurry and have a grating machine or food processor, grated carrots take only 2 minutes to cook. Use only 2 tablespoons of water; as soon as saucepan contents start to "steam" over high heat, turn heat to medium and cook for 2 minutes—no longer.

# GLAZED CARROTS

**1 pound carrots**

**½ teaspoon salt**

**3 tablespoons butter**

**½ cup liquid honey**

Utensils needed

**sharp knife**

**vegetable peeler**

**medium saucepan**

**medium frying pan**

1. Cut ends off carrots, then peel or scrape the carrots. (Use a vegetable peeler for peeling, a sharp knife for scraping.)
2. Cut carrots into 2- to 3-inch pieces.
3. Place carrots in a saucepan and add water to cover carrots. Add salt.
4. Bring water to a boil over high heat, place a lid on the saucepan, and turn heat to medium.
5. Cook carrots over medium heat until fork-tender. This will take 15 to 20 minutes.
6. While carrots are cooking, combine the butter and honey in a frying pan.
7. When the carrots are cooked, drain off all the water and add carrots to butter and honey in the frying pan. Turn heat to medium.
8. With a spoon, keep turning the carrots in the honey-butter mixture until they are well glazed on all sides.
9. Serve hot.

*Serves 4.*

# CAULIFLOWER

*Buy a head of cauliflower that is free of brown spots. You may cook it whole or break it into bite-size florets, whichever you prefer. Always soak cauliflower in salted cold water–about 1 teaspoon salt to 1 quart of water–to remove any "critters" that might be hiding. Do the same with broccoli. Twenty minutes should be sufficient.*

**1 medium cauliflower**

**½ teaspoon salt**

**1 tablespoon butter or margarine**

Utensils needed

**knife**

**large saucepan with lid**

To Cook Cauliflower Whole

1. Remove outer leaves and cut out the core (the base of the stem).
2. In a saucepan large enough to hold the whole head of cauliflower with enough space at the top to place a lid, place about 1 inch of water. Add salt. Bring water to a boil over high heat.
3. Add the cauliflower and, when water returns to the boil, cover with the lid and turn heat to medium.
4. Cook for 15 to 20 minutes, or until tender when tested with a fork (make sure you test the stem, which will be the last part to cook). Do not overcook, unless you prefer your cauliflower "mushy."
5. Drain immediately and serve topped with the butter. You may sprinkle with chopped parsley or paprika as well.

### To Cook Cauliflower Broken into Florets

1. Remove outer leaves and cut out the core. Break cauliflower into bite-size florets and cook as above, reducing cooking time by about one-half.
2. Drain immediately.

*Serves 4.*

*Variation:* Cauliflower, too, is delicious served with cheese sauce. (See the recipe for easy cheese sauce in the variation for the broccoli recipe on page 230.)

# CREAMY CAULIFLOWER

**1 large head cauliflower**

**½ teaspoon salt**

**1 carton (8 ounces) French Onion Chip Dip**

**½ cup grated Cheddar cheese**

Utensils needed

**knife**

**grater**

**large saucepan**

**round baking dish**

1. Prepare the cauliflower head as in the preceding recipe, leaving the head whole.
2. Turn oven to 350 degrees F.
3. Cook the cauliflower in salted boiling water in a large saucepan until tender. Drain.
4. Place cooked cauliflower head in a round baking dish.
5. Cover with the chip dip.
6. Sprinkle with Cheddar cheese.
7. Place in the heated oven for 15 minutes before serving. To make the cheese bubbly and brown, put the baking dish under the broiler for a few minutes before bringing to the table.

*Serves 4 to 6.*

# CORN-ON-THE-COB

*The fresher and younger the corn, the better it will taste and the shorter the cooking time. Some corn fanciers claim it is hardly worth eating if the corn is more than 12 hours from being picked! The most popular method of cooking corn is to boil it.*

**4 cobs of corn**

**4 tablespoons butter**

**Salt to taste**

**Pepper to taste**

Utensils needed

**Dutch oven or large cooking pot**

1. Remove husks and silk from corn.
2. Fill Dutch oven or other large cooking pot half full of water. *Don't salt the water!**
3. Bring water to a boil, then add the corn.
4. When water returns to a boil, cook corn for 12 minutes (use timer).**
5. Serve with butter, salt, and pepper.

*Serves 4.*

* Some cooks put 2 teaspoons of sugar in the water to sweeten the corn, but salting the corn tends to toughen it.

** If corn is "fresh from the garden," it need only be cooked for 5 minutes.

## GREEN BEANS (STRING BEANS)

*Frozen green beans, and most certainly canned green beans, cannot compare with fresh. The "French style" is the best of the frozen variety.*

**1 pound fresh green beans**

**¼ teaspoon salt**

**2 teaspoons butter or margarine**

Utensils needed

**knife**

**medium saucepan**

1. Wash green beans and cut off both tips.
2. If the beans are young and fresh, you may want to cook them whole (asparagus style). If they are more mature, break them into pieces about 1 inch in length. (You can tell whether they are young or mature by the size; the bigger they are, the older they are.)
3. Place roughly 1 inch of water and the ¼ teaspoon salt in a saucepan and bring to a boil over high heat.
4. Add beans and, when water returns to a boil, cover the pot and turn heat to medium.
5. Cook beans for 10 to 12 minutes or until fork-tender.
6. Drain immediately and add butter.

*Serves 4.*

# GREEN BEAN CASSEROLE

*This dish started appearing on dinner tables shortly after canned French-fried onions first arrived on the scene, about 25 years ago, and it is still very popular.*

**1 package (1 pound) frozen cut green beans**

**¼ teaspoon salt**

**Pinch of white pepper**

**1 can (10 ounces) cream of mushroom soup**

**1 can (2.8 ounces) French-fried onions**

Utensils needed

**medium saucepan**

**can opener**

**1½-quart casserole dish**

1. Turn oven to 325 degrees F.
2. Cook beans in a medium saucepan according to directions on package, but don't overcook; cook until just tender.
3. Drain well and rinse briefly in cold water (this helps retain the bright green color).
4. Stir salt and pepper into undiluted soup, then stir in the green beans.
5. Pour mixture into a casserole dish and sprinkle the top with canned onions.
6. Bake for 20 to 25 minutes or until heated well through.

*Serves 4 to 6.*

Note: *Drained canned green beans work as well in this recipe.*

# SAUTÉED MUSHROOMS

*Never wash mushrooms; they absorb moisture in that interesting-looking underside, and it spoils them. Either wipe with a damp cloth or invest in a mushroom brush. If the mushrooms have been sitting around for a few days and have acquired a few dark spots, peel them. They peel very easily.*

**½ pound mushrooms**

**3 to 4 tablespoons butter**

**Salt**

**Pepper**

**1 tablespoon finely chopped fresh parsley**

Utensils needed

**sharp knife**

**small or medium frying pan**

1. Clean mushrooms and cut off the ends of the stems if they look dark and gritty.
2. Slice the mushrooms, quarter them, or leave them whole, depending on how you prefer them.
3. Melt butter in the frying pan, then add mushrooms.
4. Fry gently (sauté) over medium heat, stirring occasionally, until mushrooms are tender. This will take about 5 minutes.
5. Sprinkle with salt, pepper, and chopped parsley.

*Serves 2 to 3.*

## BARBECUED ONIONS IN FOIL

**2 large onions, preferably Spanish**

**1 cup barbecue sauce (your favorite brand)**

**2 tablespoons butter**

Utensils needed

**sharp knife**

**paper towels**

**aluminum foil**

1. Heat oven to 375 degrees F.
2. Peel the onions, slice, and separate into rings.
3. Dampen a double square of paper towel (by running under the water tap briefly).
4. Lay a sheet of foil 12 to 14 inches long on your kitchen counter, center the damp towel on top, and place another piece of foil of equal length on top. (This procedure ensures that the food won't scorch or burn.)
5. Place onion rings on foil in the center, over the (hidden) damp towel.
6. Pour on barbecue sauce.
7. Dot with small pieces of butter.
8. From opposite sides, bring both thicknesses of foil together over the onions and fold over twice to seal well. Seal each end with a double fold. You have now created a sealed foil "packet."
9. Bake for 20 minutes in the oven at 375 degrees. Don't overbake or onions will become mushy.

*Serves 4.*

*Variation:* These also may be cooked on the barbecue and are terrific served with barbecued steak or a roast.

# BOILED POTATOES

*There is a variation between boiling mature potatoes and boiling new ones, so here are both methods. (It is always a good idea to remove potatoes from the plastic bag they are packaged in. Store them loosely packed in an open container in a cool place.)*

Mature Potatoes

**6 medium potatoes (about 2 pounds)**

**4 cups boiling water**

**¼ teaspoon salt**

**2 to 3 tablespoons melted butter**

**3 to 4 tablespoons chopped fresh parsley or chives**

Utensils needed

**sharp knife**

**vegetable peeler**

**large saucepan**

1. Wash potatoes well, remove sprouts and blemishes, then peel.
2. Cut into quarters and place in a saucepan.
3. Cover with boiling water; add salt.
4. Place over high heat until water comes to a full rolling boil, then turn heat to medium, cover, and cook for 20 to 30 minutes.
5. When fork-tender, remove from heat and drain well.
6. Add melted butter and parsley or chives.
7. Transfer to serving dish.

## New Potatoes

**12 small new potatoes**

**Boiling water to cover**

**¼ teaspoon salt**

**3 to 5 tablespoons melted butter**

**3 to 4 tablespoons chopped fresh parsley**

### Utensils needed

**large saucepan**

1. Scrub potatoes well. Do not peel.
2. Transfer to the saucepan and cover with boiling water; add salt.
3. Place over high heat until water comes to a full rolling boil, then reduce heat to medium, cover, and cook for 15 to 20 minutes or until fork-tender.
4. Remove from heat and drain.
5. Add melted butter and parsley.
6. Transfer to serving dish.

*Serves 4 to 6.*

Note: *The new potatoes are best served with their skins on; but if you wish to peel them, do it after cooking. A small two-pronged fork is useful as a holding tool.*

# MASHED POTATOES

*Older (starchier) potatoes are best for mashed potatoes.*

**6 medium potatoes**

**4 cups boiling water**

**¼ teaspoon salt**

**3 tablespoons butter**

**1 teaspoon salt**

**⅓ cup milk or half-and-half**

**Pepper**

Utensils needed

**knife**

**vegetable peeler**

**large saucepan**

**potato masher or electric mixer**

1. Wash potatoes well, remove sprouts and blemishes, then peel.
2. Cut into quarters and place in a saucepan.
3. Cover with boiling water; add salt.
4. Place over high heat until water comes to a full rolling boil, then turn heat to medium, cover, and cook for 20 to 30 minutes.
5. When fork-tender, remove from heat and drain well.
6. Add butter, salt, and milk to the drained potatoes.
7. Mash vigorously with a potato masher or beat with an electric mixer until smooth and creamy.
8. Add pepper to taste and transfer to serving dish.
9. Serve immediately.

*Serves 4 to 6.*

## GARLIC MASHED POTATOES

**1 whole head (not just a clove!) of garlic**

**¼ to ½ teaspoon olive oil**

Utensils needed

**scissors**

**aluminum foil**

**baking pan**

1. Remove outer skin from garlic, leaving head intact. Rub with olive oil.
2. With scissors, snip pointed ends of each garlic clove.
3. In a baking pan, cover with foil and bake at 325 degrees F for 1 hour.
4. Cool and squeeze out garlic (it will look like a paste).
5. Use the preceding recipe for mashed potatoes and add the garlic after you have mashed in the butter, salt, and milk or cream.

*Serves 4 to 6.*

Note: *If you have no time to bake the garlic, add 2 cloves of fresh garlic to the potatoes when cooking, drain, then mash the potatoes and garlic together when cooked.*

*Suggested Accompaniments:* Tossed Green Salad or Caesar Salad, crusty buns or good-quality French bread, fresh fruit plate for dessert.

# DAY-BEFORE MASHED POTATOES

*If you want to be free to concentrate on the rest of dinner, this method eliminates last-minute preparation of the potatoes. The dish may be made early in the day, or even the day before, and reheated.*

**Butter**

**3 cups mashed potatoes***

**2 eggs, well beaten**

**½ cup cereal cream (half-and-half)**

**Salt**

**Pepper**

Utensils needed

**1½-quart casserole dish**

**medium mixing bowl**

**electric mixer**

1. Preheat oven to 350 degrees F.
2. Butter the casserole dish.
3. In a mixing bowl, combine mashed potatoes with the eggs and cream, and add salt and pepper to taste.
4. Beat with an electric mixer until light and fluffy.
5. Turn into the buttered casserole dish.
6. Refrigerate until needed, but remove from refrigerator at least 1 hour before baking.
7. Bake at 350 degrees for 30 minutes.

*Serves 6.*

* See the recipe on page 248.

# PARTY MASHED POTATOES (WITH INSTANT POTATOES)

*An instant success!*

*Mashed potatoes from scratch can be a hassle for a beginner if he or she has to cope with coordinating an entire meal for guests. We have given a suggestion for "lump-free" gravy (see page 126); now here is a guaranteed "lump-free" mashed potato recipe.*

**1 large clove garlic, minced**

**3 cups boiling water (less 2 tablespoons)**

**1 teaspoon salt**

**2 tablespoons butter**

**1 cup cold milk**

**3 cups instant mashed potatoes**

**1 large egg, plus 1 yolk**

**2 good pinches (about 1/16 teaspoon) cayenne pepper**

**2/3 cup grated Cheddar cheese**

Utensils needed

**large bowl**

**1-quart casserole dish or 8 individual foil muffin cups**

1. Preheat oven to 425 degrees F.
2. Place freshly minced garlic in bottom of a large mixing bowl. Add boiling water, salt, butter, and cold milk. Stir in potato flakes gently with a fork.
3. Allow to stand for 30 seconds; then, with a fork or wire whisk, whip in the egg, the egg yolk, and cayenne pepper.

4. Spoon mixture into a l-quart buttered casserole dish and sprinkle top with grated cheese.
5. Bake at 425 degrees for 25 to 30 minutes.

*Serves 6 to 8.*

Note: *We have made these for barbecue parties, using the individual foil muffin cups (3¾ by 1⅝ inches). These are available at most supermarkets. Butter them before you add the mashed potatoes and reduce the baking time to 15 to 20 minutes. Serve the potatoes right in the cups. This amount will fill eight cups.*

## BAKED POTATOES

*Baked potatoes are delicious, nutritious, and easy. The only thing you have to remember is that you must always prick the skin of the potato before placing it in the oven. (A two-tined fork is best for this.) Most beginning cooks have a potato explode in the oven before they remember how important this little step is.*

**Baking potatoes***

**Cooking oil (optional)**

**Butter**

**Salt**

**Pepper**

Utensils needed

**scrubbing brush**

1. Heat oven to 425 degrees F.
2. Scrub the potatoes well with a brush and prick the skins with a fork to allow steam to escape from the potatoes when baking.
3. If you prefer crispy skins, rub the potatoes with a little cooking oil.
4. Bake the potatoes on a rack in the middle of the oven for 40 to 60 minutes.
5. When they are cooked, gently roll the hot potatoes with your hand on a smooth surface to make the inside light and mealy.

*Serve 1 potato per person.*

* These should be big and uniform in size so they will all be cooked at the same time.

6. Cut a criss-cross in the top of each with a sharp knife and press the sides to further open the top.
7. Drop in a spoonful of butter and salt and pepper to taste.

*Each potato serves 1.*

Hint: To *speed up cooking time, insert a 2-inch nail lengthwise into the raw potato, then bake.*

*Variations:*

1. To make baked potatoes without the skins, peel the potatoes, pour a little vegetable oil in your hand, and then roll the potato around in your hands, making sure you coat the potato well. Sprinkle generously with seasoning salt and bake on **oven rack** (no pan) at 400 degrees F for 40 to 45 minutes.
2. Foil-Baked Potatoes:

   Scrub the potatoes, dry them, then wrap individually in foil. Bake at 350 degrees F for 1½ hours.

## ROAST POTATOES

*Even a number of experienced cooks have not learned the secret of making the very best roast potatoes: You have to boil them first, but only for 5 minutes, before roasting in the oven.*

**4 medium potatoes**

**¼ teaspoon salt (plus a little extra for seasoning)**

**2 tablespoons oil**

**2 tablespoons butter**

**Salt**

**Pepper**

**Paprika**

Utensils needed

**vegetable peeler**

**saucepan**

**shallow baking dish**

1. Heat the oven to 350 degrees F. If you're making the potatoes to serve with a roast, start preparing the potatoes about an hour and fifteen minutes before serving time.
2. Peel the potatoes.
3. Place in a saucepan, cover with cold water, and add ¼ teaspoon salt.
4. Bring to a boil over high heat. Boil for 5 minutes, then remove from heat and drain well.
5. Mix oil and butter in the bottom of a shallow baking dish. Mixture should cover the pan well.

6. Place the potatoes in the pan, rolling them around to coat with oil and butter. (Or you may want to arrange them around the roast, turning once to coat with beef drippings.)
7. Sprinkle with salt and pepper to taste and paprika. The paprika is important because that is what is going to give them their golden brown appearance.
8. Bake for 30 minutes. Turn the potatoes over, and bake for a further 30 minutes or until tender when pierced with a fork.

*Serves 4.*

## SCALLOPED POTATOES

*This is an invaluable recipe. It is very easy to assemble, tastes great, and goes with just about anything.*

**2 medium potatoes**

**2 medium onions**

**1 can (10 ounces) cream of mushroom soup**

**½ soup can of milk**

Utensils needed

**vegetable peeler**

**sharp knife**

**8-inch baking dish**

**can opener**

1. Preheat oven to 350 degrees F.
2. Peel the potatoes and slice one of them crossways to cover the bottom of the baking dish.
3. Peel the onions. Slice one thinly and place on top of potato layer.
4. Slice second potato and place on top of onion layer.
5. Slice remaining onion thinly and layer over potato.
6. Stir soup and milk together and pour over potatoes and onions.
7. Bake, *covered*, for 1 hour or until potatoes are soft when pierced with a fork.

*Serves 3 to 4.*

Note: *If this is going to be served to guests, dress it up by sprinkling some chopped green pepper and chopped pimiento over the potatoes before pouring the soup over.*

# QUICK POTATOES ROMANOFF

*The Potatoes Romanoff of yesteryear demanded the tedious job of grating cold boiled potatoes, but through the magic of modern technology we are now blessed with frozen, ready-made hash browns. Try to find hash browns that most resemble grated potatoes.*

**1 package (1 pound) frozen hash browns**

**Butter for greasing**

**4 green onions**

**1 tablespoon butter**

**¼ teaspoon seasoning salt**

**1 can (10 ounces) cream of chicken soup**

**1 cup sour cream***

**1 cup grated Cheddar cheese**

**2 tablespoons grated Parmesan cheese**

**Paprika**

Utensils needed

**9-inch casserole dish**

**sharp knife**

**grater**

**can opener**

**medium bowl**

**aluminum foil**

1. Allow potatoes to thaw slightly in the bag.
2. Turn oven to 350 degrees F. Butter the casserole dish.

* Can be lowfat sour cream.

3. Chop the onions and melt the 1 tablespoon butter.
4. Combine onion, melted butter, seasoning salt, soup, and sour cream in a bowl.
5. Add grated Cheddar cheese and partly thawed potatoes.
6. Mix together well, then transfer to the buttered casserole dish.
7. Sprinkle with Parmesan cheese and a dash of paprika, if desired.
8. Bake uncovered for 35 minutes.
9. Remove potatoes from oven and let them sit for 10 to 15 minutes, covered with foil, before serving.

*Serves 4 to 6.*

*Variation:* These are excellent prepared a day ahead and refrigerated until cooking time. After sprinkling on the Parmesan and paprika, cover the casserole and place in the refrigerator. About 55 minutes before serving time, heat the oven to 350 degrees F. When indicator light shows oven has reached required temperature, uncover casserole and place in the oven to bake for 45 minutes. Serve immediately.

# OVEN-BAKED RICE

*If you are a newcomer to cooking rice, the safest method is oven-baking. It is foolproof.*

**1 cup long-grain rice, uncooked**

**2 cups boiling water**

**2 tablespoons butter**

**½ teaspoon salt**

Utensils needed

**2-quart casserole dish**

1. Heat oven to 350 degrees F.
2. Place all ingredients in a buttered, 2-quart casserole dish.
3. Cover with lid or foil and bake for 45 minutes.
4. Fluff with a fork just before serving.

*Serves 4.*

*Variation:* For more flavorful rice, dissolve 2 teaspoons instant chicken bouillon powder in the boiling water before adding.

## PERFECT BOILED RICE

*You don't need a special "rice cooker" to cook rice. Follow this simple method exactly, and you will have perfect results every time. After making it once or twice, you won't even have to reach for this book; you will know exactly how to do it. You can make it for 2 or 22 just by varying the amounts of rice and the size of the pot.*

**1 cup long-grain rice**

**1 teaspoon salt**

Utensils needed

**saucepan with tight-fitting lid**

**sieve**

1. Place rice in a medium saucepan with a tight-fitting lid and cover well with cold water. (A pot with a heavy bottom is best.)
2. Bring to a boil. As soon as water starts boiling furiously (it will look milky and frothy at this stage), drain it through a sieve. (You don't need to be told *not* to use a colander with holes bigger than the rice, right?)
3. Rinse well under cold running water.
4. Return rice to pot and cover with fresh cold water so that the water is about ½ inch above the top of the rice. (Stick your middle finger in the water until it touches the rice. The water should not come up over the first joint of your finger.) Add 1 teaspoon salt.
5. Cover pot tightly and turn heat to high. At the very first sign of steam escaping (it's important not to touch the lid), immediately turn heat to the lowest setting and cook for 30 minutes.
6. Remove from heat, fluff with a fork, and serve.

*Serves 4.*

## FOOLPROOF METHOD OF COOKING PASTA

*This method works with any kind and any amount of dry packaged pasta but not with fresh pasta.*

**Salt**

**Pasta (your choice)**

Utensils needed

**large pot**

1. Bring a large pot (spaghetti pot or soup pot) of water to a boil.
2. Add salt (2 tablespoons for 4 to 5 quarts of water).
3. Add pasta (1 pound in 4 to 5 quarts water) and stir.
4. Let water return to a boil.
5. Cover pot and turn off heat and let sit undisturbed for 30 minutes.
6. Drain and serve.

Note: *Freshly cooked pasta with just butter or olive oil, some finely minced fresh garlic, and grated Parmesan cheese (freshly grated is best) is sometimes served as a first course in Italy. Try it instead of potatoes or rice with a chicken or veal dish. If you don't have a pasta scoop (looks like a claw), get one. They're very handy. Long tongs will do but not as well.*

## CHINESE SNOW PEA PODS

*To prepare pea pods for cooking, cut the tips and tails off using scissors. If peas are a little mature, remove the stringy spine. If they are young and tender, there will be no stringy spine.*

**1 tablespoon oil**

**½ pound fresh snow pea pods**

**½ teaspoon sugar**

**Garlic**

**Salt**

**Pepper**

**Ginger**

Utensils needed

**wok or large frying pan**

1. Heat the oil over high heat in a wok or large frying pan.
2. Add the pea pods, sugar, a light sprinkling of garlic, salt, and pepper, and a pinch (as much as you can hold between your thumb and forefinger) of ginger.
3. Cover and cook for only a minute or two. You want the pea pods to be tender but still crisp.

*Serves 4 to 5.*

*Variation:* If you want to dress these up for guests, add 1 cup sliced fresh mushrooms and a small can of water chestnuts, drained and thinly sliced. Place in pan with pea pods and cook all together. If you are using frozen snow peas, rinse in cold water to thaw, then pat dry.

# BROILED TOMATOES

*A broiled tomato half is so useful when designing a meal, as much for color as for taste and convenience. Choose firm, ripe tomatoes with a good bright red color.*

**Tomatoes**

**Celery salt**

**Black pepper**

**Sugar**

Utensils needed

**pie plate or shallow baking dish**

1. Turn broiler on to preheat.
2. Wash the tomatoes and cut in half.
3. Sprinkle the cut side with celery salt (if you have no celery salt, use regular salt), black pepper (freshly ground, if possible), and a pinch of sugar on the pie plate.
4. Place under broiler for about 8 to 10 minutes, leaving oven door open. Check occasionally to make sure they are not burning.

*Serve half a tomato per person.*

*Variation:* These may be dressed up by sprinkling with grated cheese (Parmesan, Cheddar, or Swiss) or with buttered bread crumbs before placing under broiler.

## BAKED TOMATO HALVES

*These are so colorful they'll perk up any meal that seems to lack pizzazz.*

**Butter**

**2 firm large tomatoes**

**Celery salt**

**½ cup Miracle Whip**

**1 tablespoon chopped green onion**

**1 tablespoon crumbled bacon or bacon chips**

Utensils needed

**pie plate or shallow baking dish**

**sharp knife**

1. Turn oven to 325 degrees F. Butter the pie plate.
2. Cut the tomatoes in half.
3. Sprinkle the cut side with celery salt.
4. Place tomato halves in the greased dish, cut side up.
5. Divide the Miracle Whip among the tomato halves, covering the top.
6. Sprinkle with the onion and crumbled bacon.
7. Bake in the oven for 20 minutes. Do not overcook or tomatoes will lose their shape and become mushy.

*Serves 4.*

## MASHED TURNIP

*We have given the recipe for a whole turnip because, like the cabbage, it is not possible to buy one-half or part of a turnip. Don't worry, though, this dish reheats very well. Any leftover portion may be reheated in a day or two or frozen.*

**1 small turnip (about 2 pounds)**

**½ teaspoon salt**

**2 tablespoons brown sugar**

**1 tablespoon butter**

**Pinch of nutmeg**

Utensils needed

**sharp knife**

**medium saucepan**

**potato masher or food processor**

1. Peel and dice the turnip.
2. Place in a saucepan and cover with cold water.
3. Add salt and brown sugar and stir in until brown sugar is melted.
4. Turn heat to high. When water comes to a boil, cover the pot with a lid, turn heat to medium, and cook turnip until it is tender. This will take about 25 minutes. Turnip is cooked when a fork enters the turnip pieces easily.

5. Drain turnip and mash well. (This may be done in a food processor if you have one.) When turnip is well mashed, stir in butter and nutmeg.
6. Return to heat briefly to make sure it is well heated.

*Serves 4 to 6.*

*Variation:* The addition of applesauce has converted many a turnip-hater. When you have mashed the cooked turnip, add 1 cup of applesauce along with the butter and nutmeg. If you plan to add applesauce, omit the brown sugar in the cooking process.

# BAKED ZUCCHINI

*This popular vegetable is showing up everywhere–in cookies, cakes (see Carrot Zucchini Cake on page 294), soups, meat loaves and hamburger patties, to name a few. It is low in calories and high in vitamins A and C. We will give you a very simple and excellent way of preparing it so you can serve it often. Choose firm, rather small ones–6 to 7 inches in length and about 2 inches in width is a perfect size and will serve two nicely.*

**2 zucchini**

**1½ tablespoons melted butter**

**Salt**

**Pepper**

**1½ tablespoons grated Parmesan cheese**

Utensils needed

**sharp knife**

**shallow baking dish**

1. Turn oven to 350 degrees F or preheat the broiler if you are pressed for time and would prefer to broil it.
2. Wash the zucchini.
3. Leave skin on but slice both ends off and discard.
4. Cut zucchini in half lengthwise and score the cut side with a knife. (This means take a sharp knife and make slashes on the diagonal about quarter-way into the flesh; turn and do the same in the opposite direction so you have created "diamonds" about ½ inch wide.) Place in a shallow baking dish.

5. Brush the cut surface with melted butter, sprinkle with salt (seasoning salt is nice), pepper, and Parmesan cheese.
6. Place in oven for 30 minutes.
7. If you prefer to broil it, place under a preheated broiler for 10 minutes. (Remember, oven door open.)

*Serves 3 to 4.*

Note: *These timings are for tender-crisp zucchini, which is the best way to serve it.*

# ROASTED ROOT VEGETABLES

*Roasting vegetables concentrates their flavor and brings out their sweetness. You can stick to one variety or mix and match. Vegetables well suited to this method of cooking are the turnip, yam, parsnip, and carrot. When selecting carrots for baking, buy mature fat ones and cut into lengths rather than rounds.*

**2 tablespoons honey**

**1 tablespoon margarine, melted**

**¼ teaspoon salt**

**1 pound carrots, peeled and cut in ½-inch sticks**

**1 pound (1 small) turnip, peeled and cut in ½-inch sticks**

**Vegetable cooking spray**

**Onion powder (for sprinkling over top)**

Utensils needed

**large mixing bowl**

**vegetable peeler**

**sharp knife**

**cookie sheet**

**small spatula**

1. Turn oven to 375 degrees F.
2. In a large bowl, combine honey, margarine, and salt. Stir well.
3. Add vegetables and toss to coat vegetables.

4. Arrange in a single layer on cookie sheet (one that has sides, commonly referred to as a jelly roll pan) sprayed with vegetable cooking spray.
5. Bake for 1 hour or until done, stirring occasionally with a small spatula.
6. Sprinkle with onion powder.

*Serves 6 to 8.*

Note: *Vegetables are done when golden brown and soft when pierced with a fork.*

# SWEET POTATO CASSEROLE (WITH MARSHMALLOW TOPPING)

**3½ pounds (4 cups) sweet potatoes or yams***

**4 tablespoons melted butter**

**2 eggs, beaten**

**½ cup milk****

**2 teaspoons brown sugar**

**½ teaspoon salt**

**1 cup miniature marshmallows**

Utensils needed

**medium bowl**

**small saucepan**

**medium-size, shallow baking dish (1½ quart)**

1. Bake sweet potatoes or yams until tender (use the recipe for Baked Potatoes on page 253, but reduce temperature to 350 degrees F). Cool.
2. Turn oven to 375 degrees F.
3. Remove potato from skins, empty into a medium bowl, and mash. Whisk in melted butter and eggs.
4. Heat milk in a small saucepan and whisk into potatoes with brown sugar and salt.
5. Empty into medium-size, shallow baking dish (round or rectangular) and bake for 30 minutes.
6. Remove from oven and reduce oven temperature to 350 degrees F.
7. Sprinkle marshmallows evenly over top of potatoes and return to oven for 5 to 10 minutes or until marshmallows are slightly brown (watch carefully to avoiding burning!).

*Serves 8.*

* Sweet potatoes are drier than yams and the flesh is slightly yellow in color, whereas yams are a little more moist and orange in color.

** If you use yams instead of sweet potatoes, reduce the milk to 2 tablespoons (no need to heat).

# BAKED ACORN SQUASH

**1 small acorn squash**

**Salt**

**Pepper**

**1 teaspoon butter**

Utensils needed

**sharp knife**

**baking pan**

1. Preheat oven to 350 degrees F.
2. Cut squash in half and scoop out the seeds. Place in a baking pan.
3. Sprinkle cavity with salt and pepper.
4. Top with butter.
5. Bake at 350 degrees for 1 hour.

*Serves 2.*

10

# Cookies & Squares

Chocolate Peanut Clusters
Oatmeal Cookies
Bobbie's Bars
Special K Bars
Ellie's Squares
Lemon Squares
Brownies
Scottish Shortbread Fingers
Peanut Butter Cookies
"Survivor" Cookies
Butter Tarts
Rice Krispies Squares
Chocolate Chip Cookies

### Helpful Hint

Store all broken cookies and cookie crumbs in a sealed container. Make a piecrust out of them by blending $1\frac{1}{2}$ cups crushed crumbs with $\frac{1}{3}$ cup melted butter. Press into the bottom of a pie plate, chill, and then fill with pie filling.

# CHOCOLATE PEANUT CLUSTERS

*No bake–and delicious. Wise to double this recipe; they disappear quickly.*

**1 small package (6 ounces) semisweet chocolate chips**

**1 small package (6 ounces) butterscotch chips**

**2 cups peanuts, any kind**

**2 cups chow mein noodles***

Utensils needed

**double boiler**

**wax paper**

**cookie sheet**

1. Boil water in the bottom of the double boiler. (A double boiler is simply a smaller saucepan set in a larger one. In the larger one–the bottom–you have boiling water, and in the smaller one–the top–place the ingredients you want to cook. So if you don't have a proper double boiler, a smaller saucepan set in a larger one will suffice.)
2. In the top of the double boiler, melt chocolate and butterscotch chips. Remove from heat when melting is complete.
3. Add peanuts and noodles. Mix thoroughly.
4. Spread wax paper over a cookie sheet, waxed side up.
5. Drop mixture by teaspoonfuls onto wax paper.
6. Allow to set either on the counter or in the refrigerator.
7. Store in a cool place.

*Makes 16 to 20.*

* Generally found in the Chinese food section of the supermarket.

# OATMEAL COOKIES

*Always a favorite.*

1 cup brown sugar

½ cup butter or margarine, room temperature

1 egg

1 teaspoon vanilla

1 cup all-purpose flour

½ teaspoon baking powder

½ teaspoon baking soda

¼ teaspoon salt

1 cup oatmeal

Butter or cooking spray

2 tablespoons milk

Utensils needed

electric mixer

large bowl

cookie sheet

spatula

1. Turn oven to 350 degrees F.
2. With the mixer, beat together in a large bowl the sugar, butter, and egg, then add vanilla.
3. Sift together flour, baking powder, baking soda, and salt.
4. Add to first mixture and mix well.
5. Mix in the oatmeal.

6. Grease the cookie sheet with butter or cooking spray.
7. Roll into small balls and place on greased cookie sheet.
8. Dip a fork into the milk and then press the fork into the balls.
9. Bake for 12 to 15 minutes or until done (the edges will start to turn light brown).
10. Remove from cookie sheet with a spatula while cookies are still warm.

*Makes roughly 2 dozen.*

# BOBBIE'S BARS

*Here's the perfect solution for how to share three Mars bars with 12 people!*

**½ cup butter or margarine**

**3 Mars bars, cut into chunks**

**½ cup shredded sweetened coconut**

**2½ cups Rice Krispies**

Utensils needed

**medium microwave-safe bowl or medium saucepan**

**measuring cup**

**8- by 8-inch pan**

1. Melt butter and Mars bars in the microwave, covered, on high for 2 minutes or in a medium saucepan over very low heat on top of the stove. When melted, stir together to blend well.
2. Stir in the coconut and Rice Krispies, mixing gently but thoroughly.
3. Empty mixture into a buttered or sprayed 8- by 8-inch pan and refrigerate for 1 hour before cutting into squares.

*Makes 16.*

## SPECIAL K BARS

*Just the thing to pack along for hiking or camping—nutritious and energy-giving. For a healthful variation, try substituting granola for the Special K.*

**¼ cup sugar**

**½ cup corn syrup**

**¾ cup peanut butter**

**½ teaspoon vanilla**

**3 cups Special K cereal**

**Butter**

**1 package (6 ounces) semisweet chocolate chips**

Utensils needed

**small saucepan**

**large bowl**

**9-inch square baking pan**

1. Place sugar, corn syrup, and peanut butter in a small saucepan and heat gently, stirring occasionally until mixture is well blended.
2. Remove from heat and stir in vanilla.
3. Place cereal in a large mixing bowl and pour peanut butter mixture over.
4. Stir until cereal is coated with peanut butter mixture.
5. Butter the baking pan, then pack mixture evenly in pan with your fingers. (If you butter your fingers, you will find it easier to pack down.)
6. When this has cooled, melt chocolate chips over low heat, then spread on top of cereal base. Let cool before cutting in squares. Keep in a cool place.

*Makes 16 squares.*

## ELLIE'S SQUARES

*These could have been named "Skor with Ritz Bars," which describes them very well. Only three ingredients! Why didn't they have squares this easy when I was learning how to bake?*

**Butter or cooking spray**

**1 box (250 grams) Ritz crackers (original)**

**1 can (300 milliliters) Eagle brand condensed milk**

**1 package (225 grams) Hershey's Skor Toffee Bits**

Utensils needed

**9- by 9-inch baking pan**

**medium-size bowl**

1. Preheat oven to 350 degrees F.
2. Lightly butter or spray a 9- by 9-inch baking pan.
3. Coarsely crumble the Ritz crackers into a medium-size bowl.
4. Stir the condensed milk into the crumbled crackers and empty them into the pan.
5. Sprinkle the package of toffee bits over the top
6. Bake for 20 minutes.
7. Cut into squares while still warm.

*Makes 16 squares.*

Note: *For best results, use a sharp knife dipped in hot water before cutting squares, and remember to loosen around the edges. (Don't eat one as soon as you've cut them because you won't be able to stop at one!)*

# LEMON SQUARES

*Lemony!*

Crust

**1 cup all-purpose flour**

**¼ cup icing sugar**

**½ cup butter**

Utensils needed

**small bowl**

**8-inch square baking pan**

1. Turn oven to 350 degrees F.
2. Blend flour, icing sugar, and butter in a small bowl until well mixed. You may do this with an electric mixer or just use your fingers to rub the butter into the flour and sugar mixture.
3. Pat evenly into the bottom of a baking pan.
4. Bake at 350 degrees for 20 minutes.
5. Remove from oven to cool, but leave oven on.

Top

**1 cup sugar**

**Pinch of salt**

**½ teaspoon baking powder**

**2 eggs**

**2½ tablespoons lemon juice**

**1 teaspoon grated lemon rind**

**Utensils needed**

**mixing bowl**

**electric mixer**

1. Place all of the ingredients in a bowl and beat with mixer until well blended.
2. Pour over cooled crust. Return to oven for 20 to 25 minutes until top is set. When it is cooked, the top should not jiggle.
3. Remove from oven and cool.
4. When cool, sprinkle the top with sifted icing sugar and cut into squares.

*Makes 16 squares.*

## BROWNIES

*Everybody has to know how to make brownies sooner or later.*

**Butter or cooking spray**

**¾ cup all-purpose flour**

**5 tablespoons cocoa**

**1 cup sugar**

**½ teaspoon salt**

**½ cup soft butter or margarine**

**2 eggs**

**¼ cup chopped walnuts**

**1 teaspoon vanilla**

Utensils needed

**8-inch square baking pan**

**sifter**

**electric mixer**

1. Turn oven to 350 degrees F.
2. Grease and flour an 8-inch square baking pan.
3. Sift flour, cocoa, sugar, and salt together into large bowl of mixer.
4. Add all of the remaining ingredients and beat with mixer at medium speed for 3 minutes.
5. Spread mixture in the baking pan.
6. Bake in preheated oven for 30 minutes.
7. Remove pan from oven to cool, then top with the following chocolate frosting.

## Chocolate Frosting

**¾ cup icing sugar**

**¼ cup cocoa**

**2 tablespoons soft butter**

**1 teaspoon vanilla**

**1 tablespoon cereal cream (half-and-half)**

## Utensils needed

**small bowl**

1. Combine all ingredients in a small bowl and beat until good spreading consistency.

*Makes 16.*

*Topping Variations:* As soon as brownies come out of the oven, arrange 8 to 10 chocolate mint patties on top and pop back in oven for 3 minutes or until patties are soft enough to spread over entire top.

Melt a 6-ounce package of semisweet chocolate chips and ½ cup chunky peanut butter together over medium heat until smooth and spreadable. Spread on cooled brownies.

## SCOTTISH SHORTBREAD FINGERS

*Although shortbread is traditionally a Christmas treat, these are so easy to make you'll find yourself making them in July. You must use real butter.*

**¾ pound butter**

**¾ cup icing sugar**

**3 cups all-purpose flour**

Utensils needed

**large bowl**

**electric mixer**

**cookie sheet**

1. Leave butter in a large bowl out of refrigerator overnight to soften (critical to this recipe).
2. Heat oven to 325 degrees F.
3. Using an electric mixer, beat softened butter until smooth and creamy, for about 2 minutes.
4. Gradually add icing sugar, beating continuously.
5. Add flour gradually as well.
6. With clean hands, remove the soft dough from the bowl and transfer to a cookie sheet or jelly roll pan.
7. Pat and press with your fingers until dough covers pan.
8. Prick all over the surface with a fork and press the tip of a teaspoon into dough around the edges of the pan (fluting).
9. Bake at 325 degrees for 20 minutes.
10. Remove from oven and, while still hot, sprinkle lightly with granulated sugar and cut into finger-size lengths. (Cut lengthwise into four pieces, then widthwise into four pieces, then cut each section into three or four more pieces.)

*Makes 4 dozen.*

## PEANUT BUTTER COOKIES

*A glass of cold milk, a plate of these cookies, and a good book is heaven!*

**½ cup butter**

**½ cup brown sugar**

**½ cup granulated sugar**

**1 egg**

**1 cup peanut butter**

**½ teaspoon salt**

**½ teaspoon baking soda**

**1½ cups all-purpose flour**

**½ teaspoon vanilla**

Utensils needed

**large mixing bowl**

**electric mixer**

**small bowl**

**cookie sheet**

**spatula**

**cake cooler**

1. Heat oven to 350 degrees F.
2. Place butter in large mixing bowl and beat with electric mixer at medium speed until creamy. (This takes 2 to 3 minutes.)
3. Gradually beat in sugars, then egg, and beat well.
4. Beat in peanut butter.

5. Stir the dry ingredients together in a small bowl, then add the dry ingredients to the peanut butter mixture, along with the vanilla.
6. Using your hands, roll the dough into small balls about 1 inch in diameter and place them about 2 inches apart on a greased cookie sheet.
7. Flatten balls with a fork (dip the fork in a glass of cold water first to keep from sticking). Each should now measure about 1½ inches in diameter.
8. Bake for about 13 to 15 minutes or until slightly firm to the touch (the edges will start to color very slightly).
9. Remove cookie sheet from oven and transfer cookies with a spatula to a cake cooler while still warm.

*Makes about 3½ dozen.*

## "SURVIVOR" COOKIES

*So named because one whole batch of these disappeared during an episode of "Survivor."*

- 3 eggs, well beaten
- 1 cup raisins
- 1 teaspoon vanilla
- 1 cup butter or margarine
- 1 cup brown sugar
- 1 cup white sugar
- 2½ cups flour
- 1 teaspoon salt
- 1 teaspoon ground cinnamon
- 2 teaspoons baking soda
- 2 cups oatmeal
- ¾ cup pecans or walnuts, chopped

Utensils needed

- plastic wrap
- large mixing bowl
- cookie sheet

1. Combine eggs, raisins, and vanilla. Cover with plastic wrap and let sit for 1 hour. (The secret to this recipe is soaking the raisins!)
2. Turn oven to 350 degrees F.
3. In large mixing bowl, cream together butter, brown sugar, and white sugar.
4. Add flour, salt, cinnamon, and baking soda to sugar mixture. Mix well.

5. Blend in the egg–raisin mixture, then the oatmeal and chopped nuts. Dough will be stiff.
6. Drop by heaping teaspoons onto ungreased cookie sheet or roll into small balls, place on cookie sheet, and flatten slightly with fork dipped in milk or water.
7. Bake for 10 to 12 minutes or until lightly browned.

*Makes 5 to 6 dozen.*

# BUTTER TARTS

*These are so good still slightly warm from the oven, but they will keep well at room temperature for 2 days. If there are any left after a couple days, it's best to refrigerate or freeze them.*

**12 tart shells, about 3 inches in diameter (can be found in frozen food section at supermarket)**

**2 eggs**

**2 teaspoons vanilla**

**2 tablespoons milk**

**1½ cups brown sugar**

**¼ cup melted butter**

**½ cup raisins**

Utensils needed

**cookie sheet**

**medium mixing bowl**

**cooling rack**

1. Place oven rack at lowest position and turn oven to 375 degrees F.
2. Leave shells in foil containers and place on cookie sheet (one with sides in case there is a spill).
3. In medium mixing bowl, whisk eggs with vanilla and milk until blended.
4. Stir in brown sugar and butter until evenly mixed.
5. Distribute raisins equally over bottoms of shells.
6. Pour egg mixture equally into shells over top of raisins.
7. Bake on bottom rack for 20 to 25 minutes or until filling is bubbly and top is slightly crusty.
8. Cool on a rack.

*Makes 12 tarts.*

# RICE KRISPIES SQUARES

*You can find this recipe on the back of a box of Rice Krispies* except *when you are looking for it. And since this is such a universal favorite, it's a good idea to have a constant source. (Just don't lose this cookbook!)*

**¼ cup butter or margarine**

**4 cups miniature marshmallows**

**½ teaspoon vanilla extract**

**6 cups Rice Krispies**

Utensils needed

**3-quart saucepan**

**13- by 9-inch baking pan**

1. Melt butter or margarine in a 3-quart saucepan.
2. Add marshmallows and cook over low heat, stirring constantly, until marshmallows are melted and mixture is well blended.
3. Remove from heat and stir in vanilla.
4. Add Rice Krispies and stir until well coated with marshmallow mixture.
5. While still warm, press mixture evenly into a lightly buttered 13- by 9-inch baking pan.
6. Cut into squares when cool or as needed.

*Makes 24 two-inch squares.*

# CHOCOLATE CHIP COOKIES

2½ cups all-purpose flour

1 teaspoon baking soda

1 teaspoon salt

1 cup butter (or margarine), room temperature

¾ cup white sugar

¾ cup brown sugar, firmly packed

1 teaspoon vanilla

2 eggs

2 cups semisweet chocolate chips

1 cup chopped walnuts (not too finely chopped), optional

Utensils needed

small or medium bowl

large mixing bowl

measuring spoons

cookie sheet

1. Turn oven to 375 degrees F.
2. Combine flour, baking soda, and salt in a small or medium bowl.
3. In large mixing bowl, beat together the butter, white and brown sugars, and vanilla until creamy.
4. Beat in the eggs, one by one.
5. Add flour mixture and blend.
6. Stir in chocolate chips and nuts by hand.
7. Drop by rounded teaspoonfuls onto ungreased cookie sheet. Do not flatten.
8. Bake for 8 to 10 minutes or until done.

*Makes 2 dozen.*

# 11

# Cakes



## Helpful Hints

1. When baking in glass dishes, decrease the oven temperature 25 degrees to prevent overbrowning.
2. Cakes should be thoroughly chilled before frosting.
3. A cake is done when it shrinks slightly from the sides of the pan, or if it springs back when touched lightly with your finger.

# CARROT ZUCCHINI CAKE

*Carrot cake's popularity has kept increasing, as has the variety of recipes. The following recipe must surely be the very latest and most nutritious, with such additions as zucchini* and *co-conut* and *whole wheat flour. If you have no whole wheat flour, use all-purpose flour.*

**2 eggs**

**1 cup sugar**

**⅔ cup oil**

**¾ cup all-purpose flour**

**½ cup whole wheat flour**

**1 teaspoon baking powder**

**1 teaspoon baking soda**

**1 teaspoon cinnamon**

**¾ teaspoon salt**

**1 cup grated carrot**

**1 cup grated zucchini, peeled first**

**½ cup shredded coconut**

Utensils needed

**9-inch square baking pan**

**large bowl**

**medium bowl**

**grater or food processor**

**electric mixer**

1. Turn oven to 350 degrees F.
2. Grease and flour a 9-inch square baking pan or spray with a vegetable cooking spray.

3. Beat eggs with sugar in a large bowl until frothy.
4. Gradually beat in oil.
5. Combine dry ingredients in a medium bowl, add to first mixture in the large bowl, and beat together until well mixed. Batter will be a little on the thick side.
6. Add carrot, zucchini, and coconut. Beat with mixer until well blended.
7. Pour into prepared pan.
8. Bake in the preheated oven at 350 degrees for 35 to 40 minutes or until top springs back when lightly touched.
9. Leave in pan. Frost when cool with Cream Cheese Frosting (see page 296).

*Makes 1 cake.*

## CREAM CHEESE FROSTING

**1 small package (4 ounces) cream cheese, at room temperature**

**¼ cup butter**

**2 cups icing sugar**

**1 teaspoon vanilla**

**1 teaspoon grated orange rind**

Utensils needed

**electric mixer or wire whisk**

**rubber scraper or frosting knife**

1. Beat cream cheese and butter together with mixer until creamy.
2. Beat in icing sugar, vanilla, and orange rind until creamy. Spread on cake.

## LOWFAT SPICE CAKE

*There are two nice features about this cake: reduced calories and easy preparation.*

**1 cup raisins**

**1 teaspoon cinnamon**

**½ teaspoon allspice**

**1 teaspoon mace**

**1 teaspoon baking soda**

**1 cup boiling water**

**1 cup sugar**

**1 cup mayonnaise, regular or Miracle Whip Light**

**1 teaspoon salt**

**2 cups flour**

Utensils needed

**small mixing bowl**

**large mixing bowl**

**9- by 9-inch pan**

1. Turn oven to 350 degrees F.
2. Put raisins, cinnamon, allspice, mace, baking soda, and boiling water in a small mixing bowl and stir to mix. Let sit and cool to room temperature.
3. While mixture in the small bowl is sitting, stir sugar, mayonnaise, salt, and flour together in a large mixing bowl then stir in the contents of the small bowl.

4. Empty into a greased and floured 9- by 9-inch pan and bake for 40 minutes or until a toothpick inserted in the center comes out clean.

*Makes 1 cake.*

Note: *This cake really does not need to be iced, but if you have a sweet tooth that needs satisfying, try Myrna's Fudge Icing* *(see page 299).*

## MYRNA'S FUDGE ICING

**1 cup light brown sugar**

**3 tablespoons margarine or butter**

**3 tablespoons cream (heavy is best, but it works with light cream as well)**

**Pinch of cream of tartar**

Utensils needed

**medium saucepan**

1. Stir all the ingredients except cream of tartar together in a medium saucepan and mix well.
2. Bring to a boil over high heat. When it reaches a rolling boil, reduce heat to low and cover.
3. Cook for exactly 3 minutes.
4. Remove from heat and add cream of tartar. Stir vigorously, then pour over cake.

Note: *This also will ice a Bundt cake or a 9- by 13-inch cake.*

## LARGE CHOCOLATE CAKE

*If you like your chocolate cake moist, heavy, and "chocolatey," we're sure this will be a long-standing favorite.*

**1 package (6 ounces) Jell-O Chocolate Pudding–not instant**

**2½ cups milk**

**1 package (18 ounces) devil's food cake mix**

**Butter or cooking spray**

**1 cup semisweet chocolate chips**

Utensils needed

**large saucepan**

**9- by 13-inch cake pan**

**spatula**

1. Heat oven to 375 degrees F.
2. Using a large saucepan, make pudding according to package directions but use 2½ cups milk instead of the quantity given on the package.
3. When pudding is cooked, remove pot from heat and add cake mix. Stir until blended.
4. Grease or spray the cake pan.
5. Transfer batter to the cake pan, distributing the batter evenly and smoothing the top.
6. Sprinkle chocolate chips over top.

7. Bake for 25 minutes or until the top of the cake springs back when touched with a finger. (Oven *must* have reached 375 degrees before you put the cake in; watch indicator light.)
8. Immediately after removing the cake from the oven, smooth the melted chocolate chips over with a knife (to resemble icing), though you may prefer to leave them as is for a bumpy effect. Tastes good both ways.

*Makes 1 cake.*

# THE ABSOLUTE BEGINNER'S CHOCOLATE CAKE

*The easiest chocolate cake around—no bowl to wash and no saturated fat! Ellie helps her mom make this, and Ellie is only 3 years old!*

**1½ cups flour**
**1 teaspoon baking powder**
**1 teaspoon baking soda**
**4 tablespoons unsweetened cocoa**
**1 cup sugar**
**1 tablespoon vanilla**
**1 tablespoon white vinegar**
**1 tablespoon canola oil**
**1 cup plus 1 tablespoon warm water**

Utensils needed

**9- by 9-inch baking pan**
**wooden spoon**
**rubber scraper or frosting knife**

1. Preheat oven to 375 degrees F.
2. Place flour, baking powder, baking soda, cocoa, and sugar into a greased 9- by 9-inch baking pan. Mix well.
3. Make three holes (or wells) in the mixture.
4. In the first hole, put the vanilla; in the second hole, put the vinegar; and in the third hole, put the oil.
5. Pour the warm water over all and mix well with a wooden spoon, making sure you get the corners.
6. Bake for about 20 to 25 minutes or until the center springs back when lightly touched.
7. When cool, ice with Chocolate Frosting.

Chocolate Frosting

**3 tablespoons soft butter or margarine**

**1¼ cups confectioner's sugar**

**1 teaspoon vanilla**

**¼ cup unsweetened cocoa**

**4 teaspoons hot (not boiling) milk or light cream***

Utensils needed

**electric mixer**

**small bowl of electric mixer**

**rubber scraper or frosting knife**

1. Place the soft butter or margarine in the small bowl of your mixer and gradually beat in confectioner's sugar, vanilla, and cocoa with the hot milk or cream. (Add more milk if icing is too thick, more confectioner's sugar if it is too thin.)
2. When smooth, spread over top of cooled cake.

*Makes 1 cake.*

* For a mocha-flavored frosting, substitute hot coffee for the milk or cream.

## NO-BAKE FRUITCAKE

*One of the biggest problems one is faced with when making a fruitcake is timing. Ovens vary a bit in temperature and it is difficult to give an exact baking time. If you overcook the fruitcake it is dry and crumbly, and undercooking produces a "doughy" mess. After many weeks of experimenting, we finally solved the problem–don't bake it!*

**1 pound marshmallows**

**1 cup sherry**

**1 pound raisins**

**1 pound chopped candied fruitcake mix**

**3 cups chopped pecans**

**1 cup shredded coconut**

**1 box graham cracker crumbs (14 ounces)**

Utensils needed

**two 9- by 5-inch loaf pans**

**double boiler**

**large bowl**

1. Line two loaf pans with foil and set aside.
2. Place marshmallows in the top of a double boiler. (See page 275 for a description of a double boiler.) Set this over simmering water in the bottom part of double boiler and, stirring occasionally, leave marshmallows over heat until melted. Stir in sherry.

3. Place all remaining ingredients in a large bowl. When the melted marshmallows and sherry are thoroughly combined, pour onto the dry ingredients and mix well. You may want to use your hand for this since batter will be slightly heavy and sticky.
4. Divide mixture evenly between the loaf pans. Pack down well and cover with foil. Store in a cool place for about 1 week before slicing and serving.

*Makes 1 cake.*

Note: *A microwave may be used for melting the marshmallows.*

## COCONUT CAKE

- **2 eggs**
- **1 cup brown sugar**
- **⅛ teaspoon baking soda**
- **¼ cup plus 1 tablespoon all-purpose flour**
- **1 teaspoon vanilla**
- **1⅓ cups shredded coconut**
- **2 tablespoons butter**

Utensils needed

**medium bowl**

**8-inch square baking pan**

1. Turn oven to 325 degrees F.
2. Break eggs into a bowl and beat with a fork until lemon-colored throughout. This will take only about 20 to 25 vigorous strokes with the fork.
3. Add the brown sugar, baking soda, flour, and vanilla; mix well with the fork–about 40 additional strokes. Stir in the coconut.
4. Place butter in the baking pan. When the red oven light has gone out, indicating that oven is at the right temperature, place the pan in the oven until butter has melted.
5. Remove pan from oven and tilt back and forth to distribute melted butter evenly.
6. Empty contents from bowl onto melted butter. Press gently to spread evenly but *do not stir.*
7. Bake for 25 minutes.

*Makes 1 cake.*

## LEMON YOGURT CAKE

- 1 package lemon cake mix
- 1 package (3¾ ounces) Jell-O Lemon Instant Pudding
- 4 eggs
- 1 cup unflavored yogurt
- ¼ cup lemon juice
- ¼ cup water
- Oil or baking grease
- Flour

Utensils needed

- electric mixer
- angel food cake pan*

1. Turn oven to 350 degrees F.
2. Place all ingredients into large bowl of mixer and beat thoroughly for 5 minutes with mixer at medium speed.
3. Grease and flour the cake pan.
4. Empty batter into cake pan and bake in preheated oven for 45 to 55 minutes.
5. Remove from oven and cool before removing from pan. Frost or glaze with either of the following toppings.

* If you have no angel food cake pan, use a 9- by 13-inch cake pan and bake at 350 degrees for 35 to 45 minutes or until top springs back when lightly touched with fingers. It won't be as showy as the higher round cake but it will taste exactly the same.

## Lemon Butter Cream Icing

- **3 tablespoons butter**
- **1 teaspoon grated lemon rind**
- **¼ teaspoon salt**
- **2½ cups icing sugar**
- **4 tablespoons cereal cream (half-and-half)**
- **1 teaspoon vanilla**

Utensils needed

**large bowl**

**electric mixer**

1. In a large bowl, blend the butter, lemon rind, and salt.
2. Add the icing sugar gradually, ½ cup at a time, beating between each addition.
3. Add the cream and vanilla. With electric mixer at high speed, beat until the icing is creamy.
4. Spread on cooled cake.

## Glaze

*Easier than making an icing and adds a finishing touch to the cake.*

- **½ cup sugar**
- **2 tablespoons lemon juice**
- **½ cup orange juice**

Utensils needed

**small saucepan**

1. Combine ingredients in a small saucepan.
2. Place over medium heat and stir until sugar is dissolved.
3. Pour while still warm over cooled cake.

*Makes 1 cake.*

# 12

# Desserts

Baked Apples
Flaky Apple Dumplings
Bachelor's Apple Pie
Apple Crisp
Peach Crumb Pie
Chocolate–Peanut Butter Pie
Tipsy Torte
Chocolate-Dipped Strawberries
Lemon Chiffon Pie (the Easy Way!)
My First Mousse
Pecan Pie
Blueberry Cheesecake
Butterfinger Angel Food Dessert
Strawberry Shortcake
Ice Cream Pie
Pumpkin Pie

## Helpful Hints

1. Peeled, cored, and sliced apples (like potatoes) will not discolor if immediately placed in cold salted water or lemon or lemon-lime soda.
2. Spoon a little undiluted frozen orange juice over cut-up fresh fruit for a deliciously refreshing fruit salad.
3. For a "hurry up" chocolate sauce, melt some Hershey milk chocolate with almonds over hot water, then stir in a tablespoon of rum. Serve warm over vanilla ice cream.

# BAKED APPLES

*This is one of the few desserts you would bother making just for yourself, and then you would make two, one to serve hot with your dinner and the other to have cold with the following night's dinner. These are strictly family fare. If you want to dress baked apples up for guests, follow the recipe for Flaky Apple Dumplings on page 311.*

**Apples**

**Brown sugar**

**Butter**

**Cinnamon**

**Whipping cream**

Utensils needed

**apple corer**

**shallow baking dish**

1. Turn oven to 375 degrees F.
2. Wash and core the apples and place in a baking dish.
3. Cut skins at the top of the apple in an X to prevent skins from bursting.
4. Fill cavities with brown sugar. Top with a dab of butter and a sprinkle of cinnamon.
5. Fill baking dish with water to a depth of ¼ inch.
6. Bake for 45 to 50 minutes or until apples are tender.
7. Pour cream (unwhipped) over the apples just before serving.

*Make 1 apple per person.*

# FLAKY APPLE DUMPLINGS

*Absolutely delicious but quite filling. Would suggest it follow a rather light meal (or 50 push-ups!).*

**1 package frozen puff pastry dough, thawed (14½ ounces)**

**4 large apples**

**½ cup raisins**

**2 tablespoons chopped nuts**

**1½ cups brown sugar**

**1 cup water**

**Sweetened whipped cream (optional)**

Utensils needed

**rolling pin**

**apple corer**

**shallow baking dish**

**small saucepan**

1. Make sure the pastry dough is thawed. Heat oven to 400 degrees F.
2. On a clean kitchen countertop, roll dough into a 16-inch square.
3. Cut into four squares.
4. Peel and core the apples, placing one on each square.
5. Mix raisins and nuts and fill apples.
6. For each square, moisten the corners with a fingertip dipped in water, then bring two opposite corners up over the apple and press together. Repeat with the other two corners so that the apple is sealed in an envelope of dough.

7. Place the apples in an ungreased baking dish.
8. Combine brown sugar and water in a saucepan over medium-high heat, bring to boiling, and pour around the dumplings in the dish.
9. Bake at 400 degrees for 40 minutes.
10. Spoon the syrup over the dumplings a few times during baking period.
11. Best served warm with sweetened whipped cream but also good cold the next day.

*Serves 4.*

## BACHELOR'S APPLE PIE

*This could have been named "One-Dish Apple Pie" because that is all you need.*

**1 cup Bisquick baking mix**

**4 tablespoons soft butter**

**3 tablespoons boiling water**

**5 medium apples**

**½ cup brown sugar**

**1 teaspoon cinnamon**

**½ cup sour cream**

**2 tablespoons butter**

Utensils needed

**9-inch pie plate**

**apple corer**

1. Heat oven to 350 degrees F.
2. Mix the Bisquick, soft butter, and water in the pie plate (a fork works well), then press it evenly on the bottom and around the sides of the pie plate.
3. Cut apples into four sections; remove peel, then core (a melon baller is a marvelous tool for this). Slice each quarter section into thin slices.
4. Place apple slices on top of Bisquick crust you have made.
5. Combine the brown sugar, cinnamon, and sour cream and distribute as evenly as you can over the top of the apples.
6. Dot with butter cut into little pieces.
7. Bake for 30 minutes.
8. Serve while still warm, with a scoop of vanilla ice cream.
9. Leftovers are great served cold the next day, but we bet you won't have any.

*Makes 1 pie.*

# APPLE CRISP

*A great way to use up those apples that are "going."*

**Butter**

**1 cup brown sugar**

**¾ cup all-purpose flour**

**1 teaspoon cinnamon**

**½ cup butter or margarine**

**5 apples**

Utensils needed

**8-inch square baking pan**

**small bowl**

**pastry cutter***

1. Heat oven to 375 degrees F.
2. Butter the baking pan.
3. Mix together brown sugar, flour, and cinnamon in a small bowl.
4. Cut in butter with the pastry cutter until the mixture is the consistency of coarse bread crumbs.
5. Peel and slice the apples.
6. Combine ¼ of the crumb mixture with the sliced apples.
7. Place in the buttered baking pan. Sprinkle the top with remaining crumb mixture.

* If you don't have a pastry cutter, use two knives or a potato masher with large holes.

8. Bake for 45 minutes.
9. Serve warm with cream, whipped cream, or ice cream.

*Serves 6.*

*Variation:* Rushed? Substitute a can of apple pie filling for the apples, and either cut out or cut down the amount of sugar, depending on the sweetness of your tooth.

# PEACH CRUMB PIE

*Even though we consider ourselves to be experienced cooks who make not a bad pastry, we've always used the convenient ready-made pie shells for this particular recipe; that way this pie really comes under the heading of the yummiest jiffy dessert you'll ever make.*

**9-inch ready-made, frozen, deep-dish pie shell**

**½ cup all-purpose flour**

**¼ cup white sugar**

**¼ cup brown sugar**

**½ teaspoon cinnamon**

**¼ cup butter**

**½ cup chopped walnuts or pecans**

**1 can peaches (14 ounces)**

Utensils needed

**small bowl**

**pastry cutter or 2 knives**

**can opener**

1. Thaw the pie shell. (Do not prick the crust.)
2. Turn oven on to 450 degrees F.
3. In a small bowl, mix the flour, sugars, and cinnamon.
4. Using a pastry cutter if you have one, or simply two knives, cut the butter into the flour mixture until butter pieces are about the size of a pea.
5. Spread approximately half of this mixture in the bottom of the pie shell.

6. Add the chopped nuts to the rest of the mixture in the bowl.
7. Drain liquid from the peaches and slice them. (Either discard or drink the drained juice; you will not need it for this recipe.)
8. Arrange the peach slices in the piecrust.
9. Top with remaining flour mixture.
10. Bake at 450 degrees for 10 minutes, then turn oven down to 350 degrees and continue baking for 20 minutes.
11. Serve warm with a scoop of vanilla ice cream.

*Serves 5 to 6.*

# CHOCOLATE–PEANUT BUTTER PIE

*Definitely what we'd suggest the day before the diet begins. This dessert keeps very well in the freezer–ready to be brought out for an emergency (which could be a sweet snack attack!).*

Crumb Crust

**1¼ cups graham wafer crumbs or chocolate wafer crumbs**

**¼ cup brown sugar (packed)**

**⅓ cup margarine or butter, melted**

Utensils needed

**9-inch pie plate**

**can opener (unless you use bottled syrup or sauce)**

Filling

**1 quart (about 4 cups) chocolate ice cream**

**1 cup peanut butter (smooth)**

**1 cup Hershey's Chocolate Syrup**

**1 cup peanuts**

1. Mix together the crumbs and brown sugar.
2. Add melted butter or margarine.
3. Stir well with a fork, then pat firmly into bottom and up the sides of a buttered 9-inch pie plate.
4. Place pie shell in freezer to set firmly.
5. Meanwhile, take ice cream out of freezer to soften *slightly* (for easier spreading).
6. When pie shell is well chilled, spoon half of ice cream into shell and pat down firmly.
7. Return pie to freezer until ice cream is set.

8. Remove from freezer and spread with a thin layer of peanut butter (about ½ cup).
9. Drizzle with half the chocolate sauce.
10. Sprinkle with half the peanuts.
11. Repeat the layers.
12. Return to freezer.

*Makes 1 pie.*

To Serve: *Remove pie from freezer 10 minutes before cutting. Add a dollop of whipping cream to each portion or heat additional chocolate syrup to pour over. (If waistlines will allow, by all means use both!)*

## TIPSY TORTE

*Great fun to serve. Only you will know the ease with which it was made, and your friends will have a great time guessing about the ingredients. We've served this to guests numerous times and have yet to find a guest who has guessed right!*

**1 pint whipping cream**

**⅓ cup Tia Maria or Kahlùa**

**½ cup milk**

**1 package chocolate chip cookies**

**1 square semisweet chocolate, shaved (grated)**

Utensils needed

**electric mixer or hand beater**

**small bowl**

**8-inch springform pan or 9-inch square glass baking dish**

**grater**

1. Whip the cream with chilled beaters until stiff. This takes about 2 minutes with an electric mixer and a bit longer with a hand beater.
2. In a small bowl, combine the liqueur and milk.
3. Butter the springform pan or square baking dish.
4. Dip each cookie quickly in the liqueur-and-milk mixture, but do not soak.
5. Set cookies side by side in the bottom of the pan until it is covered. Fill in empty spots with dipped broken cookies.

6. Spread a layer of whipped cream over the cookies.
7. Repeat layers until the pan is full or all the cookies are used, ending with the whipped cream.
8. Top with a sprinkling of shaved chocolate. (Grating the chocolate against a potato peeler is a quick and easy way to get shaved chocolate.)
9. Refrigerate at least 6 hours or overnight.

*Serves 6 to 8.*

## CHOCOLATE-DIPPED STRAWBERRIES

*These make a great "finger food" dessert. Don't wash the berries. It is illegal to spray berries with insecticide, so they are perfectly safe to eat. If there is any sand or surface dirt, just wipe with a clean cloth.*

**Whole strawberries, with stems**

**1 large package semisweet chocolate chips (12 ounces)**

**6 tablespoons butter or margarine**

Utensils needed

**wax paper**
**cookie sheet**
**double boiler***

1. Have clean, perfect strawberries ready on a sheet of wax paper. Have the wax paper, in turn, sitting on a cookie sheet since you have to transport the berries to the refrigerator.
2. Melt the chocolate chips in the top of a double boiler over hot (not boiling) water.
3. Stir in the butter and keep stirring until butter is melted and well mixed with the chocolate.
4. Dip strawberries in the chocolate, swirling to coat evenly, but leave the very top of the berry, below the stem, uncovered. It looks more attractive to see a bit of the berry. Work quickly before the chocolate hardens, and start with the biggest berries because they will need deeper chocolate than the smaller ones.

* For a description of a double boiler, see page 275.

5. Place berries on the wax paper after dipping and refrigerate until serving time.

Note: *If some of the berries are without stems, insert a cocktail pick into the area where the stem would be to enable you to hold the berry for dipping.*

*Variation:* Strawberries Dipped in Sour Cream and Brown Sugar: Another popular "finger" strawberry dessert is made by having a platter of strawberries served with two small bowls in the center of the table, one filled with sour cream and the other with brown sugar. One first dips the strawberry into the sour cream, then into the brown sugar.

# LEMON CHIFFON PIE (THE EASY WAY!)

**1 can condensed milk**

**1 can frozen lemonade concentrate, thawed (6 ounces)**

**2 tablespoons fresh lemon juice**

**½ teaspoon grated lemon rind (optional)**

**1 carton Cool Whip (16-ounce size, which is 2 cups)**

Utensils needed

**can opener**
**wire whisk**
**9-inch pie plate**
**grater (optional)**

1. Combine above ingredients with a wire whisk and empty into a 9-inch graham cracker crust (see the recipe for Crumb Crust in Chocolate–Peanut Butter Pie recipe on page 318; reserve 2 tablespoons crumbs for sprinkling on top of pie).
2. Place in freezer until serving time (for a minimum of 3 hours).

*Serves 6.*

## MY FIRST MOUSSE

*This is almost as simple as making a bowl of Jell-O but transforms a box of Jell-O into a rich-tasting dessert that you can serve to family or guests. It is one of those desserts that you can make after work and have ready to serve right after dinner.*

**1 package of Jell-O* (small size, 85 grams)**

**1 cup boiling water**

**1 pint vanilla ice cream**

Utensils needed

**medium bowl**

1. In a medium bowl, dissolve the Jell-O in the boiling water, making sure you stir until all Jell-O is dissolved.
2. Immediately cut in the ice cream and stir until melted.
3. Chill in the refrigerator for 1 hour. You can make it more than an hour ahead of time because it "sits" well.

*Serves 4 to 6.*

* Our favorite flavor is the raspberry Jell-O, but you can vary the Jell-O powders to suit the occasion: raspberry for Valentine's Day, lime for St. Patrick's Day, lemon for Easter, and so on.

# PECAN PIE

*If you don't have to worry about the pastry, pecan pie is likely one of the easiest pies to make. If you cheat and use a ready-made frozen pie shell, this filling is so good no one will notice that the piecrust is not homemade. The secret of a good pecan pie is not to beat the filling with a rotary beater, only with a fork.*

**9-inch ready-made, frozen, deep-dish pie shell**

**3 eggs**

**1 cup sugar**

**¼ teaspoon salt**

**1 cup dark corn syrup**

**¼ cup melted butter**

**1 cup pecans**

**Whipped cream**

Utensils needed

**medium-size bowl**

**fork**

1. Thaw the pie shell.
2. Heat the oven to 375 degrees F.
3. In a medium-size bowl, beat the eggs with a fork.
4. Add the sugar, salt, syrup, and melted butter. Beat with a fork until well mixed.
5. Add pecans.
6. Transfer to the unbaked pie shell. Bake for 45 minutes or until a knife inserted into the filling comes out clean.
7. Serve with whipped cream or, better still, whipped cream with a dash of brandy in it.

*Makes 1 pie.*

## BLUEBERRY CHEESECAKE

*Not as "cheese-cakey" as most cheesecakes but creamy and rich.*

Crust

**2¼ cups graham wafer crumbs**

**⅓ cup sugar, white or brown**

**⅓ cup melted butter**

**Dash of cinnamon**

Utensils needed

**medium mixing bowl**

**electric mixer**

**9- by 13-inch baking dish**

**can opener**

1. Combine all ingredients for the crust in a mixing bowl.
2. Mix together well and pat into a baking dish.
3. Refrigerate while you prepare the filling.

Filling

**1 envelope Dream Whip**

**1 package cream cheese (8 ounces)**

**1 can blueberry pie filling (19 ounces)**

1. Prepare Dream Whip according to package directions.
2. Add cream cheese and beat with a mixer until light and fluffy.
3. Remove crumb crust from refrigerator. Spread cheese mixture on top to cover crust completely.

4. Spread blueberry pie filling on top of cheese layer.*
5. Refrigerate 2 to 3 hours before serving.

*Makes 1 cheesecake.*

Note: *Do not substitute whipped cream for the Dream Whip; it won't have enough body and it becomes watery after a while.*

*Variations:*

1. Add 1 cup frozen blueberries to the pie filling before spreading it.
2. Add a teaspoon of grated orange rind to the crumb crust for an extra bit of zip.
3. Try different toppings. Cherry and pineapple pie filling are excellent substitutes for the blueberry.

* The pie filling will be easier to apply if the cheesecake is placed in the freezer long enough to firm up–30 minutes to an hour.

## BUTTERFINGER ANGEL FOOD DESSERT

*Such a cinch to whip up but absolutely scrumptious, so be ready for compliments. Best made the night before.*

**1 ready-made, 10-inch angel food cake**

**4 Butterfinger bars***

**1 pint whipping cream**

Utensils needed

**cake plate**

**small bowl**

**electric mixer or hand beater**

1. Slice the cake in half so you have a top and bottom layer. Set the bottom layer on a cake plate.
2. Break up the Butterfinger bars into small pieces but not crumbs in a small bowl.
3. Whip the cream with chilled beaters until stiff (about 2 minutes with a mixer and a bit longer by hand).
4. Add Butterfinger pieces to whipped cream and stir.
5. Spread the whipped cream mixture on the top of the bottom layer of the cake, set the remaining layer on top, then ice the top and sides of the cake, using all the cream mixture.
6. Chill in the refrigerator for at least 4 hours.
7. An extra, crumbled Butterfinger bar may be sprinkled on top of the cake as an attractive garnish.

*Serves 10 to 12.*

* If Butterfinger bars are not available use Crispy Crunch bars.

## STRAWBERRY SHORTCAKE

*High on the list of favorite desserts. Everyone has his or her own preferred way to serve it. Here is one simple way.*

**2⅓ cups Bisquick baking mix**

**3 tablespoons sugar**

**3 tablespoons melted margarine or butter**

**½ cup milk**

**2 small cartons fresh strawberries**

**1 tablespoon sugar**

**1 carton whipping cream (½ pint)**

**1 teaspoon sugar**

**1 teaspoon vanilla**

Utensils needed

**medium bowl**

**8-inch round cake pan**

**small deep bowl**

**electric mixer or hand beater**

1. Heat oven to 425 degrees F.
2. Combine baking mix, 3 tablespoons sugar, margarine, and milk in a bowl. Mix until a soft dough forms.
3. Spread evenly in an ungreased round baking pan.
4. Bake 15 to 20 minutes or until golden brown.
5. Wash, hull, and slice the strawberries. Sprinkle with 1 tablespoon sugar.

6. When cake is baked, remove from oven. Cool in the pan on a rack for 10 minutes, then cut into six wedges.
7. Pour whipping cream into a chilled deep bowl. Whip with mixer until cream starts to thicken. Add 1 teaspoon sugar and the vanilla and continue beating until cream starts to form stiff peaks. (Having the beaters chilled hastens the procedure.)
8. To serve, split each wedge in half. Set the bottom half on a dessert plate and spoon some of the strawberries over it, then place the other half on top and spoon on more strawberries. Mound whipped cream on the very top.

*Serves 6.*

*Variations:* Most supermarkets carry ready-made sponge cakes, angel food cakes, or individual sponge cakes, all of which may be used as your cake base. If you are a whipped cream addict, you may like to whip an additional carton of whipping cream and put whipped cream between the layers as well.

# ICE CREAM PIE

*Make this as far ahead as you like. A big hit with young and old alike.*

**½ pound peanut brittle**

**1 quart vanilla ice cream**

**1 bottle butterscotch syrup (such as Smucker's)**

Utensils needed

**10-inch pie plate**

**plastic wrap**

1. Crush the peanut brittle.
2. Soften the ice cream enough to mix in the peanut brittle. Don't fold in all of the peanut brittle—save some to decorate the top, about ½ cup.
3. Press the mixture into a lightly buttered pie plate, sprinkle with "saved" peanut brittle, cover with plastic wrap, and store in the freezer until ready to use.
4. At serving time, heat the butterscotch syrup and pass separately with wedges of ice cream.

*Serves 8. For smaller servings, see variation below.*

*Variation:* Form ice cream into balls (an ice cream scoop is helpful for this purpose) and roll in crushed peanut brittle or chopped pecans. Freeze balls on a cookie sheet; when solidly frozen, transfer to plastic bags for storing in the freezer. These are handy to have on hand, but make sure you have a bottle of syrup on the shelf.

# PUMPKIN PIE

*Did you know that canned pumpkin makes better pies than freshly cooked pumpkin?*

2 large eggs, slightly beaten

1 can pumpkin (14 or 16 ounces)

¾ cup sugar

½ teaspoon salt

1 teaspoon cinnamon

½ teaspoon ginger

⅛ teaspoon ground cloves

1½ cups evaporated milk

9-inch unbaked pie shell (must be the deep-dish version)*

Whipped cream

Utensils needed

can opener
large bowl
electric mixer

1. Turn oven to 425 degrees F.
2. Place all the ingredients (except pie shell and whipped cream) in the order given into large mixer bowl, and beat with mixer until well mixed.
3. Pour into pie shell and bake for 15 minutes.

* A commercial pie shell does not hold as much filling as one you could make yourself, so any leftover filling may be poured into individual custard cups and baked along with the pie.

4. Reduce oven temperature to 350 degrees and continue baking for 45 minutes or until a knife inserted in the center of the pie filling comes out clean.
5. Let cool.
6. Garnish with whipped cream.

*Makes 1 pie.*

# An Introduction to Utensils

If you have the following utensils, you can make anything and everything in this book.

## ESSENTIAL

Following are things you'll definitely need to make most of the recipes in this book:

*Baking pans and dishes:* You'll need three different measurements: 8- by 8- by 2-inch, 9- by 9- by 2-inch, and 13- by 9- by 2-inch. Metal pans are called "pans." Corning Ware, Pyrex, and such. are called *dishes* or *casserole dishes*. All of the baked goods—cakes, squares, and so on—have been tested in metal pans. We highly recommend Teflon-coated pans and have found that, after the first few uses, it is best to spray before each use with one of the vegetable oil sprays such as Mazola No-Stick or Pam. For pans requiring greasing and flouring, Baker's Joy is excellent.

*Bowls for mixing:* These come in three sizes—large, medium, and small—and all are necessary.

*Broiler pan:* This comes with a rack and is usually found in every oven other than microwave or convection.

*Cake cooler:* You may use the rack from your broiler pan as a cake cooler.

*Can opener*

*Casserole dishes:* Casserole dishes come in all shapes and sizes—round, square, oblong, oval—usually with a lid. It's best to make sure you have both a 1-quart and a 2-quart.

*Colander:* This is sometimes called a strainer.

*Cookie sheet*

*Double boiler:* Two pots designed to fit together so that simmering water in the lower pot will gently cook the contents in the upper pot.

*Dutch oven:* A large-capacity, heavy-bottom pot with a tight-fitting lid. Usually holds 4 quarts.

*Egg beater*

*Fork:* A two-tined, long-handled fork that is for safe handling of hot foods.

*Frying pan or skillet:* It is best to get two sizes; three is even better: small, medium, and large.

*Grater*

*J-cloth:* A fine, mesh disposable dishcloth resembling cheesecloth. Also called HandiWipes.

*Knives:* Make sure you have small paring knives and French chefs. Get good-quality knives.

*Loaf pan:* One 9- by 5-inch loaf pan will do.

*Measuring cups*

*Measuring spoons*

*Mixing bowls:* See *Bowls for mixing.*

*Muffin tins*

*Oven mitts or pot holders*

*Pie plate*

*Potato masher:* This also is useful for dicing a large quantity of boiled eggs should you be making egg salad sandwiches.

*Pots or saucepans:* You'll need three sizes: small, medium, and large.

*Rolling pin*

*Salad bowl*

*Spatulas:* You'll need both a rubber and a metal spatula.

*Spoons:* It's best to make sure you have at least one wooden spoon, one slotted spoon, and one long-handled metal spoon.

*Vegetable peeler:* This may be used to core apples as well.

## NOT ESSENTIAL BUT HELPFUL

These are things you can pick up along the way that will make cooking much easier, but they are not absolute necessities:

*Blender or food processor:* Go for the food processor—beg, borrow, or steal if necessary.

*Cake pan:* Buy at least one 8-inch round (you will need two of these to make a layer cake). You may want to buy an angel food cake pan, but all of the recipes in this book may be baked in square or oblong pans. (See also *Baking pans and dishes.*)

*Custard cups:* Four is enough to start with.

*Double boiler*

*Dutch oven*

*Egg slicer:* This is handy for dicing eggs and slicing mushrooms. To dice eggs, turn lengthwise and then widthwise.

*Electric mixer*

*Garlic press*

*Kitchen shears*

*Meat thermometer*

*Molds:* You should invest in two molds—a 4-cup and a 6-cup.

*Soufflé dish*

*Spring form pan:* One 8-inch springform pan.

*Wire whisk*

*Wok*

# How to Measure

It is important that ingredients be measured properly.

*All dry ingredients:* These include baking powder, baking soda, and salt. Be sure to use the proper measuring spoons and level off with a straight-edged knife.

*Butter or margarine:* It is helpful to know that most of these are marked in some way. If you buy the 1-pound boxes, their contents are divided into four individual packages and each of these packages is ½ cup. If you need ¼ cup, divide the package in half; should you need 1 cup, use two packages.

*Flour:* Flour usually comes presifted. Spoon it loosely into a dry measuring cup (no lip) and level it off with a straight-edged knife. Should you have only the liquid measuring cup (comes with a lip), make sure the flour is level.

*Sugar:* White sugar is treated the same as flour, but *brown sugar* is firmly packed.

It also is helpful to remember the following measures:

2 tablespoons = ¼ package
4 tablespoons = ½ package
8 tablespoons = 1 package

*Authors' Note:* We have mentioned many brand names throughout this book. This is not really an endorsement, as there are comparable brands available. These just happen to be our current favorites!

# Index

# INTERNATIONAL CONVERSION CHART

These are not exact equivalents: they have been slightly rounded to make measuring easier.

## Liquid Measurements

| *American* | *Imperial* | *Metric* | *Australian* |
|---|---|---|---|
| 2 tablespoons (1 oz.) | 1 fl. oz. | 30 ml | 1 tablespoon |
| ¼ cup (2 oz.) | 2 fl. oz. | 60 ml | 2 tablespoons |
| ⅓ cup (3 oz.) | 3 fl. oz. | 80 ml | ¼ cup |
| ½ cup (4 oz.) | 4 fl. oz. | 125 ml | ⅓ cup |
| ⅔ cup (5 oz.) | 5 fl. oz. | 165 ml | ½ cup |
| ¾ cup (6 oz.) | 6 fl. oz. | 185 ml | ⅔ cup |
| 1 cup (8 oz.) | 8 fl. oz. | 250 ml | ¾ cup |

## Spoon Measurements

| *American* | *Metric* |
|---|---|
| ¼ teaspoon | 1 ml |
| ½ teaspoon | 2 ml |
| 1 teaspoon | 5 ml |
| 1 tablespoon | 15 ml |

## Weights

| *US/UK* | *Metric* |
|---|---|
| 1 oz. | 30 grams (g) |
| 2 oz. | 60 g |
| 4 oz. (¼ lb) | 125 g |
| 5 oz. (⅓ lb) | 155 g |
| 6 oz. | 185 g |
| 7 oz. | 220 g |
| 8 oz. (½ lb) | 250 g |
| 10 oz. | 315 g |
| 12 oz. (¾ lb) | 375 g |
| 14 oz. | 440 g |
| 16 oz. (1 lb) | 500 g |
| 2 lbs | 1 kg |

## Oven Temperatures

| *Farenheit* | *Centigrade* | *Gas* |
|---|---|---|
| 250 | 120 | ¼ |
| 300 | 150 | 2 |
| 325 | 160 | 3 |
| 350 | 180 | 4 |
| 375 | 190 | 5 |
| 400 | 200 | 6 |
| 450 | 230 | 8 |